free
to be me

a journey through fear to freedom

betty robison

LIFE OUTREACH PUBLICATIONS

Library of Congress Cataloging-in-Publication Data
Robison, Betty.
   Free to be me: a journey through fear to freedom / Betty Robison. p. cm.
   ISBN 978-0-9800638-8-2 (sc)
   1. Robison, Betty. 2. Christian biography—United States.I. Title.
BR1725.R6247 A3 2003
277.3'082'092—dc21

Printed in the United States of America

16 15 14 13
11 10 9 8

*To the Lord Jesus, Who gave me life and freedom;
to my husband, James, my greatest encourager;
and to our three children, Rhonda, Randy, and Robin,
who God has used to reveal His abounding grace and
who have blessed us with eleven wonderful and very
special grandchildren!*

Acknowledgments

There was a time in my life when I could never have imagined writing the acknowledgments for a book I wrote. I am thrilled to be publicly thanking many who have meant so much to me and have been such a big part of the positive changes in my life. Above all, I'm grateful for a great and wonderful God who loves me and didn't give up on me, even through my times of resistance to His will.

First of all, I'd like to thank my husband, James, who, like God, never ceases telling me I am special. We have now been married for 50 years, and he has always been—and still is—my greatest encourager. Our story is still being written, but we have learned so much about each other and about our journey with the Lord. To this day his love and confidence in me have never wavered. James, thank you for seeing what I believe God wanted to do in my life and for helping me grow and become strong. Thank you for also recognizing that I do have gifts from God and can do anything with His help because "with God all things are possible." Thanks for your love and support, and for continually building me up and making me feel safe and secure.

I also have overwhelming gratitude for our three children—Rhonda, Randy, and Robin—for being inde-scribable blessings in my life. Our precious daughter

Robin has gone to be with the Lord, and while her passing was sorrowful, I will treasure the memories more each day. What a blessing it has been to be their mother, a calling God put deep in my heart.

We have been blessed with eleven grandchildren, and each one of them truly brings joy and delightful energy into our family. Their beautiful and different personalities are so unique and precious to me. And I have learned from watching them grow. They are real jewels.

I also acknowledge my parents, Victor and Margaret Freeman, who both have gone on to be with the Lord. Thank you, Mom and Dad, for giving me life and a home; and even though our home-life wasn't perfect, it was evident that your love for me, my sisters, and brother was pure.

I must also mention my list of wonderful friends who have an awesome influence on my life. Chere Fleming Wilpitz, without knowing it, affected me positively when we were children. She showed me what a true friendship was like. I believe she was one of the first people God put in my path to encourage me. Lynda Simmons was like a sister to me during those years when our children were so small. Then there is Jody Claytor, with her gentle, caring heart. My dearest friends, Susan Ellison and Janis Harris have stuck by me through thick and thin. All of these ladies are the greatest listeners, comforters, and friends I've ever known. Also, Sarah Hall and Julia McKay shared their hearts, homes, and coffee with me every time my husband left to go preach for days at a time. These friends have lifted me up and carried me when I didn't feel as though I could stand. Proverbs 20:6 says, *Many will say they are loyal friends, but who can find one who is truly reliable?* (NLT). Thank you, ladies—you have truly been faithful.

And finally, a very special thanks to Jeanne Rogers. Jeanne, there is no possible way to thank you adequately for your selfless devotion in assisting me in the writing of this book. You have poured your heart and time into this project, working so diligently to help me express my heart. You have cried with me and laughed with me as I recalled such significant experiences in my life. "Thank you," will never be enough, but THANKS, anyway.

CONTENTS

Have you ever . . .

+ felt insecure?
+ been afraid to fail?
+ wondered why your passion for life has dimmed?
+ felt plain and ordinary when others around you seem to be shining stars?

Do you think . . .

+ you have to be "good" for God to love you?
+ you have to "do" in order to be someone?
+ you can't "rock the boat" in your relationships or you'll lose those you love?
+ you don't measure up to others?
+ you're ugly, invisible, or inadequate?
+ you don't deserve God's mercy because of who you are or what you've done?

If any of these secret thoughts apply to you, you're not alone. But it can certainly feel that way. I know, for I have struggled personally with each of the above thoughts and feelings.

For years I lived in a prison of fear and self-doubt, paralyzed by the false thinking that God would love me only if I was good, which to me translated as being busy "doing something" for him. And yet no matter what I did, it was never enough. I was still plain, ordinary Betty—the middle, invisible, inadequate child who grew up feeling like she never measured up.

This book is my life story—the story of how a young, shy girl from Texas moved from the shackles of fear to a true freedom in Christ. Although the journey has taken me many years, and it's not entirely over yet (God is continually refining me, thankfully), I can now say boldly that I finally have discovered the "good news": God loves us and accepts us *just as we are, right now.* We don't have to be perfect to come before him. In fact, he is waiting for *us,* longing for intimate, two-way communication. And he longs to show us how to break out of our individual prisons—negative thoughts, past behaviors, destructive patterns—for only then can we be fully free. Free to be the unique persons he has created us to be. And, most of all, free to pursue, without hindrance, the kind of loving relationship he longs to have with us as his children.

So yes, this is my story. I offer it humbly. It is a story of hope . . . and I hope that within its pages you will glimpse a little of yourself, and perhaps any patterns, thoughts, or behaviors that are holding you back from experiencing the depth and wonder of what God has prepared for you. Most of all, I pray that you will discover, as I did, the glorious freedom that can come only from knowing Christ and walking daily, moment by moment, with him.

The Lord gives freedom to the prisoners.
   —*Psalm 146:7*

CHAPTER ONE

I'DADDY

IF SOMEONE ASKED ME WHO WAS MOST IMPORTANT TO ME AS a child, I'Daddy, my maternal grandfather, would first come to mind. Perhaps it was because my summers with I'Daddy and Granny near Lufkin, Texas, were the times I felt most loved, most free to be me in those early days. Or maybe it was because my grandparents showered us with the time, love, and attention that I longed for so desperately as the middle child in a family of six.

Although I was too young to recall all the details of those summers, I only knew that I wasn't invisible at I'Daddy and Granny's, like I felt I was at home. And I didn't feel inadequate or ugly either. Surprisingly, my mother told me that I even became a camera "ham." She said I always wanted to be out front.

For instance, I can imagine a scenario like this one summer day. . . .

Dodging my older brother Pete's elbows, I squeeze into the center, inside of my sisters, Marjorie and Helen.

"Betty Catherine," Granny teases, "you're a little camera bug."

We push and shove until I'm off to the side, and our grandmother doesn't have a good view. So again I slip in front to pose myself in the center. When my feet are firmly planted on the bottom step, my grandfather folds his newspaper and directs his attention to us from the lawn chair behind Granny.

"I'Daddy, make Betty stop trying to get my spot," Pete yells. While learning to talk, Pete had been the one who had first called Grandfather "I'Daddy." Since then the name has stuck; we all use it.

"Settle down, kids, and stand farther back so Granny can get you all in the picture," I'Daddy says.

In her usual, feisty manner Granny approaches the steps and takes charge posing us. She tugs and straightens our clothes. Then, spitting on her finger, she pastes down Pete's stray hairs while he tries to squirm away. "Now stay put, and stand still. I want this to be a good picture for my album."

"Ettie," I'Daddy interrupts, "put Betty back where she was. Her height looks better in the middle. Besides, I want to see those big dimples."

I gloat as Granny follows his instructions and gives me the prominent position. I love having my picture taken. My boldness to pose out front or in the center of a picture surprises everyone. In most competitive situations with my brother and sisters, I wouldn't be so forceful.

After the photo is taken and Granny begins to turn the handle to rewind the film, I rush to my grandfather and lean on his knee. "I'Daddy, do you think we got some good pictures?"

"Well, the sunlight was just right. That last pose looked good, and your dimples really smiled at me. Granny will give your momma a picture when we get them developed."

A short distance from the house was my grandparents' country store. I often watched as I'Daddy pumped gas into a car. The driver got out and talked while I'Daddy cleaned the windshield and checked under the hood.

I positioned myself where I could watch my grandfather and hopefully have his attention when he finished servicing the car. I'Daddy made me feel special—something I was starved for. All he had to do was mention my dimples, and they magically appeared. What caused dimples, anyway? I didn't know, but they seemed to be the only part of my appearance that deserved praise. I had overheard my mother say, "I asked that doctor why Betty's head was so big and her body so small when she was born. She seemed so out of proportion compared to Marjorie and Pete."

After that I paid special attention to any comparison made about me. Comments offered to inspire me to improve often had the opposite effect. I wondered how many things could be wrong with me. I never heard negative remarks about my older sister, Marjorie's, appearance. Helen was the baby of our family but only fourteen months younger than I was. Her cuteness invited special attention from my parents and Granny. Pete, as the only boy, was special too. And then there

3

was me, the girl who wasn't special in any way . . . at least that's what I thought.

I watched I'Daddy remove the heavy nozzle from the man's car and hook it back in place. The man counted dollar bills that he took from his wallet as my grandfather wiped gasoline from his hands with a red cloth snatched from his back pocket. The man gestured with the money in his hand, and they had a hearty laugh as I'Daddy replaced the gas cap.

When the man started his car, I stayed a safe distance away. After the customer left, I hurried toward I'Daddy. "Can I put the money in the cash register?" He counted the dollar bills and handed them to me with a gentle pat on my head. I gripped them securely in both hands and walked as close to him as I could. I loved the smell of gasoline on his hands and clothing.

The cash-register drawer opened with a loud *ding*. He lifted me up, and I placed the bills on top of the few collected earlier that day. Together we closed the drawer, my legs dangling as he supported me for the strong push to close it firmly. Then, instead of letting me slip down to the floor, he lifted me shoulder level for a big hug.

When I was with I'Daddy, the negative feelings about myself disappeared. It was clear, even to a young child, that he loved me. He always seemed to have time for me, offering nothing but kind, encouraging words.

Whenever I could, I rode with him in his old pickup to do business in the town of Lufkin. I'Daddy drove *fast*. In the stores people made jokes about his crazy driving. I wasn't sure what they meant, but I also overheard comments on his business dealings: "Tom Miller is a no-nonsense kind of guy." Those trips were special for me because all around town his many friends greeted us cheerfully, and riding anywhere with him was a thrill.

During the day my grandfather did carpentry work while Granny ran the store and filling station. They worked long hard hours, but somehow during most of each summer, they managed to keep all four of us Freeman kids while Mother and Daddy focused on their jobs. We played in and around the store every day, taking turns pretending to be the store owner and customers. We even borrowed a variety of merchandise from the shelves to make our game more realistic. Of course Granny kept us near her, since she was responsible for the store and its real customers.

Our eyes never tired of looking at the variety of sweets displayed on their country store's wooden shelves. While most children could only dream of such a privilege, snacks such as peanut patties, Three Musketeers, and chocolate soda pops were available to us daily. What a privilege—the other customers had to pay for their treats and we got ours free. However, Granny carefully monitored the snacks we consumed each day. Although she was a tiny woman, we never put anything over on her.

One of our favorite treats, after playing out in the Texas heat, was digging for a Coca-Cola from the large, ice-packed soda pop box. As we sat under a shade tree outside the store, we would drop salted peanuts into each bottle. Then we would swirl the nuts around, searching the dark liquid to keep count. Or we covered the opening and shook the bottle. It's a wonder we didn't choke on a peanut when we guzzled the fizzing Coke. Once our drink was gone, we would pound the bottom of the bottle while holding the narrow glass top to our lips. We easily could have chipped our teeth or cut our mouths in the pursuit of trapped peanuts. But children don't think about such things, and we were fortunate.

At the end of his day of working as a carpenter, I'Daddy would relieve Granny at the country store so she could prepare supper in their home next door. Once the store closed and he came to the house, he would drop wearily into his rocking chair.

When I knew he was home, I was never far away. I anticipated my name being called and I wasn't disappointed.

"Betty Catherine!"

In a flash I was by his side. It was an honor to be chosen.

"Would you comb the sawdust out of my hair, honey?" I'Daddy would run his fingers through his coarse black hair, freeing it of surface wood shavings. Then I would grab the big nylon comb and work tediously to remove the rest. I knew I had done my job well if he fell asleep with my comb's gentle strokes.

When the traces of carpenter's work had been removed from his hair, I'Daddy would hand me a nail file and let me clean his fingernails. I never saw it as a dirty job but worked patiently to earn his approving smile. I welcomed the opportunity to express my love in a way that seemed effortless for me.

Now I realize that my days with I'Daddy provided an emotional connection to the strongest father figure in my life. I drew stability and strength from him. When I was in his care, I was never lost in the middle.

The vacations with our grandparents were wonderful, but near the end of the summer all of us would become homesick for our parents and our home in Pasadena, Texas, a suburb of Houston. When a long-distance call from Mom announced a potential day for their arrival, Granny went right to work mending, cleaning, and pressing our well-worn summer clothes.

Several days before their expected arrival, I would sit in the tree swing near the road next to the store. Pete, Marjorie, and Helen played nearby, as they had all summer. I occupied the swing for hours, hoping for a surprise, perhaps early, arrival. The swing gave me a clear view down the narrow road outlined by tall pine trees. When a car emerged from the distortion of heat waves rising from the pavement, I studied its shape and color. My heart pounded when I thought my parents were driving toward me. When the car, similar in color and size, drove past or turned in front of the gas pumps for service, I fought back tears. I wouldn't leave that swing until dark.

After several days of watching for my parents, I noticed Granny and I'Daddy bringing the suitcases out to the porch. I could hear Pete and my sisters playing with a doodlebug in the sand near the house.

"I asked you children to stay out of the dirt," Granny reminded. "Don't you want to be clean for your momma and daddy?"

I knew my brother could care less about being clean, but I cared. I checked my favorite blue sundress, one my mother had sewn for me. It was spotless, and the lace trim stood up crisply on my shoulders from Granny's starching. I wanted to stay neat and clean so Mother would notice me.

I wanted to be the first to see the peach-colored car, and the first to greet them when they pulled in front of the house. I rehearsed my words, envisioning the hugs and kisses. Maybe my father would pick me up and hug me the way I'Daddy did. . . . At least that was my dream. But I'm sorry to say that I don't remember that kind of affection from my dad. Although I felt his love for me, it seemed he struggled to express it physically. I found out much later that he, too, grew up feeling insecure.

CHAPTER TWO

DON'T ROCK THE BOAT

THE GOOD-BYES TOOK LONGER THAN USUAL THAT TEXAS summer of my childhood. Even though I was torn between staying with my grandparents, where I received so much affection, and returning to my real home and life with Mother and Daddy in Pasadena, I never told anyone. I didn't want to rock the boat.

That would become a pattern of my life.

When my mother and father arrived to take us back home, all of us drank a cold soda from the pop box in the store and then visited on the porch. When the conversation grew long, we four kids gave up on leaving and resorted to playful amusement around our loaded car. I was thrilled when the adults finally moved their conversation from the porch toward us. Once we realized they would continue talking by the car, we were forced to play somewhere else. Occasionally Daddy warned us not to wander off. "We're 'bout to leave," he would say.

But Mom never wanted to leave as quickly as Daddy. Although Daddy didn't talk much, he had a way of letting her know he wanted to move along before the temperature reached its usual ninety-nine degrees.

Our departure hit the final stretch as Mom and Daddy loaded us into our sun-baked car with no air conditioner. Granny gave each of us a farewell hug and kiss, reminding us to be good children. I received my kiss from I'Daddy and held on to his neck, savoring his affection before I slumped into the backseat with Pete and Marjorie. Helen sat in front between my parents, which meant she would soon be asleep in the comfort of my mother's lap.

I knew I'Daddy and Granny would watch our car from the edge of their gravel drive until we turned and headed toward Pasadena. It was a tradition. So I leaned out and waved my good-bye until Mom told me to get my head and arms back in the car and sit in the seat. Even though Pete took up more than his share of the backseat, I didn't complain. I just squeezed in beside Marjorie.

Other than the summers spent with Granny and I'Daddy, my brother, sisters, and I were seldom apart from our parents. Life was simple—at least it appeared that way to me. My father drove our only car to the Champion Paper Mill, where he clocked in eight hours, five days a week. Whenever he could, he caught a ride with another millworker so Mother could have the car for our needs. She was a full-time mom until we were older; then she got a job at the mill for some extra income.

We were a middle-class family, living in a small, two-bedroom house where my two sisters and I shared a room, and Pete slept on a daybed in the dining room. The house had a small kitchen and one tiny bathroom with a gas heater in it. We didn't know we were crowded. We thought our house was the largest on the block.

We did everything together. Every meal was eaten as a family around our dining table. When errands needed to be run, the kids went too. We often sang in the car and played typical car games such as I Spy.

Camping was our favorite family outing. Most trips took us into the East Texas pine country that my father loved. He would set up in a campground near a river that provided many adventures. Exploring and swimming were our favorites. The extremely hot temperatures allowed us to sleep outdoors—a real treat for us kids.

As with most families, life was not without mishaps. At the age of ten, while roller-skating, I broke my arm and had to wear a cast for six weeks. The doctor removed the hard protective plaster a few days before we left for vacation but advised caution with my activities. I was excited! I would get to swim in the river with my brother and sisters.

On my first visit to the river, I worked my way down the steep bank to join the other swimmers. To steady myself on the slippery bank, I planted my foot at the base of a protruding root. When it gave way, I landed on my fragile arm, breaking it in the same place. My parents drove a great distance to the nearest hospital, and my arm was once again put into a cast. Upon our return to our campsite, the family vacation continued. But I spent my days on the riverbank, watching everyone else have fun. For twelve weeks I could be only an observer of recreational activities, wearing a collection of signatures on the white plaster to prove I had been there. That memory stands out as one of my greatest childhood disappointments.

Although my parents weren't wealthy, they managed to provide enough toys and entertainment that we never felt deprived. At Christmas many presents were marked "To Betty and Helen, From Santa Claus." Since my sister and I were so close in age, we shared our toys regularly, simply taking turns. Although I was slightly older, Mom often dressed us alike, and people thought we were twins.

But our personalities were poles apart. I was self-conscious and afraid to disappoint people. Helen was strong willed, outgoing, and confident. When I would suggest things to do, she wouldn't listened. Instead she daringly planted her feet and said, "I won't do it." Even when I tried to reason with her she stood her ground until I surrendered, "Okay . . . *Okay!*"

Helen and I were great playmates, settling our own arguments as soon as I gave in to her. Otherwise, we knew Mom had several effective ways of settling them for us, including spanking. But she was never abusive with her correction. After the spanking, we were put to bed for a nap—in the same bed. In no time our anger turned to giggling.

Sometimes Mother made us face each other and say,

"I love you." Once forced to speak the words, even through pouting and pursed lips, our anger was disarmed. As we sat staring into each other's eyes, a smile provoked a returning snicker. Soon we were laughing and playing again.

Helen and I also joined Pete and Marjorie in games with neighborhood friends. Warm days and evening twilight inspired the neighborhood games of Red Rover and Mother, May I. After dark we chased fireflies and played hide-and-seek until we were called in for baths.

Our parents encouraged us to play outdoors, and I think that forced us to play more creatively. One of Pete's favorite games was Tarzan and Jane. He made up our jungle scenes, directing and casting players the way he envisioned it. Pete was Tarzan and our neighbor, a girl he liked, was Jane. I always had to be the monkey.

Usually I went along with my brother's and sisters' suggestions. Confident in their leadership, they created so much fun for all of us. Besides, I didn't want to cause any trouble.

It took me many years to realize that I'm a lot more like Daddy. Quiet and gentle, he seemed to prefer following my mother's lead. Although she never wanted to be the decision maker, her strong, outgoing personality made it that way. But it wasn't easy for her. After all, l'Daddy had led his family and communicated his feelings easily. My mother had grown up respecting him as the head of their home. Then she married Daddy, who was so different from her father. When Daddy wouldn't take the lead in their home, I think Mom felt forced into that role. After she assumed the responsibility, he relaxed and went along with most things she decided. He never wanted to rock the boat.

But there was one place where Daddy wouldn't follow my mother's lead—in church attendance. Mom saw to it that we regularly attended the little neighborhood Baptist church, where she taught Sunday school. My daddy seldom went with us. All of us kids had to be there early to assist Mom's class preparations. Then we attended our own Sunday school class, the morning service, Sunday evening training union classes, Wednesday prayer meeting, and Thursday evening evangelism and visitation. I guess all that was too much for Daddy.

To his credit, however, Daddy didn't keep us back from any church activities. And I never loved him less for not going with us. Somehow, even as a young child, I sensed that my father wanted to let his feelings out and communicate his love, but something held him back. He couldn't verbally express or physically demonstrate his affection the way I'Daddy did. According to Mom, it was because Daddy didn't receive affection from his parents and, as a result, might not know how to give it. Later Mom told us that Daddy felt called to the ministry when he was young, but his father angrily forbid it. She figured that huge disappointment, with no communication of love, made him bury his emotions. At some point Daddy disqualified himself from serving God altogether.

Although I don't remember Daddy embracing us or saying, "I love you," I still felt his affection. I saw his heart through his actions as a devoted provider, making enough money to keep Mom at home with us every day during our preschool years. And his participation in our recreation—including the many camping and fishing trips—said a loud "I care about you" to us kids over the years. I understood him; I accepted that he needed to love us his way. But when I was six, I wished he would lift me into his lap to snuggle with him. I wished I could clean his fingernails for him, as I did for my grandfather, or do any kind of service that could help me express my feelings for him.

I longed for the courage to tell my father what was in my heart. But the words were trapped somewhere inside, and I was afraid to let them out.

15

CHAPTER THREE

BEING GOOD

As I grew up, I observed something that puzzled me. No adult males in my life demonstrated a love for God or chose to lead spiritually. They weren't evil men; all worked hard to provide for their families. But the women clearly took the initiative in spiritual matters. It was from them that I absorbed what I felt to be the truth: that in order to please God and people, you had to be good. And that meant proving you were godly in every way.

A close look at my mother's family tree revealed that many branches had godly females. Only one godly male was included—a great-grandfather who was a circuit-riding preacher. But with that one exception, it was the women who went to church, read their Bibles, and sang favorite hymns around the house while doing chores. They were the ones who taught their children to pause and give thanks before digging into their food. I remember hearing, "God can work a miracle," as a matriarch of our family stated her faith. The oldest women voiced prayers of faith using *thee* and *thou* as they called for God's power to save and heal. It was their voices that boasted of God's faithfulness to meet a financial need. "Well, God got us through the Great Depression, didn't he?"

During the summers at Granny's, we traveled down a long dirt road in the country to worship at a small Methodist church. Nothing about the people or the service was stiff or formal except for the respectful language they used to talk to God. Men reverently removed their hats when they entered the wooden-plank building. Each side wall of the rectangular-shaped structure featured a row of tall glass windows. Unpadded, dark wood pews provided the seating for the congregation. A kneeling rail crossed the front of the church with an opening that allowed the pastor to enter and offer Communion. When my grandmother described "old-time religion," I always pictured this church.

Granny also told tales about her mother, Granny Massey. I couldn't imagine a woman being more audacious than my wiry little grandmother, but the stories she told about her own mother revealed the strong inspiration in her life. When relatives gathered, children and adults were fascinated by the life tales of our God-fearing ancestor.

"She didn't live in wealth as the world knew it, but she was rich with God's blessings," Granny explained. "Once my mother gave away her last pair of shoes to someone she felt needed them more. She believed the

Lord would supply her needs, so she'd give away her last nickel if God told her to do it."

"Granny, tell us the story about worshiping God on the rail," we begged.

Granny chuckled as if she were back in time, sitting on the church pew, watching. "She was too old to be walking up there on top of that prayer rail, but when she got to praising the Lord, no one could talk her down. On occasion Granny Massey got full of the joy and climbed up on that narrow beam at the altar. With her hands lifted, she walked back and forth, shouting praises and singing loudly."

As I listened to Granny's dramatic descriptions, I imagined my mother as a young child, watching her grandmother display such gallant worship at that church. I couldn't picture my mother walking on a prayer rail, but I believed she was courageous and served God with as much sincerity. It was clear she too was the greatest spiritual influence in the lives of us children. She taught us Bible stories and led us to sing together, harmonizing on hymns and gospel melodies she loved. Her stories and songs created a peaceful world where I retreated, hoping to encounter God. Although I was too shy to have my great-grandmother's daring spirit, I shared her heart's desire.

But my brother and sisters were the ones who received some of her courage in their temperaments. They did well at everything they attempted. Timid and insecure, I became their follower. When I tired of partici-pating in their creative play, I withdrew to a secluded

19

place. Our house sat on a corner and had a large side yard. I loved to go there and think about Jesus. Mom had described Jesus' love as unique and special for each child. My child's mind interpreted that as *I am not just one in the middle or one in a great population of children. I am special to God.* That was important to me.

When no one was home to watch, I would dress up in a pink ballerina costume with matching ballet slippers, given to me by a friend who took dance lessons. The isolated area of the yard became my stage. Lost in my own little world, I twirled around the grassy floor, imitating dance movements I had seen. I sang songs to Jesus, creating my own words and melodies. I freely expressed my love and hoped it would please him. In many ways, loving the Lord was like loving l'Daddy, because he too made me feel special. I needed to be alone with Jesus and do something for him that revealed my heart.

Years later Mom confessed how she had spied on me from the door, watching curiously. I'm glad I never saw her. Self-conscious and embarrassed, I probably would have quit. In her wisdom my mother kept the side yard a safe place for me to perform. It was the one activity I had courage to do on my own. It was the one place where I was free to be me.

The early spiritual training I received from Mom and church, however, made me think I had to be good or Jesus wouldn't love me. In my mind any request of the church demanded my obedience, and that obedience would hopefully inspire Jesus to love me more.

The church gave individual boxes of offering envelopes to every family member. Proud to have my own box, I took my offering commitment very seriously. Each week I pulled an envelope from my supply. Small squares across the bottom listed the activities I was expected to perform. I regularly check-marked Bible study, prayer, attendance, visitation, and offering, indicating my service to God had been done faithfully. The report-card type envelope put a load of responsibility on me, but I was passionate about keeping up the good marks.

21

I dared not cheat like other kids, who marked the square when they hadn't done the activity. I believed they disguised themselves as righteous Christians for the deacons who inspected the envelopes and counted the offering, but I knew they couldn't fool God. Afraid to be dishonest, I marked only the duties I had truthfully done. I pushed myself to do the work and earn a perfect score.

Church played such a big part in our lives that we kids often conducted our own service at home on Sunday afternoon. When we went to Granny's house, the living room became our sanctuary. Her pedestal table was the perfect child-height pulpit, and the sofa made a padded pew. Pete assumed the role of pastor as we sang, prayed, and read Scripture. He preached a short sermon and gave an invitation to the three of us sitting in the congregation. As the altar call began, Pete shouted, "You need to repent!" I went forward as the sorrowful sinner, desiring to get right with God. Of course it was a child's make-believe game, but I was sure our enactments were true to the Christian life. I couldn't bear the thought of making a mistake, so I kept a repentant heart at all times.

I loved church and got caught up in all the activities there. It was the place I felt I could excel.

But scoring 100 in my schoolwork didn't go as well. Thankfully, throughout my school years, my teachers seemed to understand and gave me passing grades for consistent effort. They knew what I know now: on daily assignments, I did well; however, testing terrified me.

I dreaded the end of each six weeks, when I had to take my report card home. Mom would congratulate and reward Marjorie's high grades, holding her up as an example. She never meant to be hurtful, but using my sister as inspiration reinforced my lack of confidence. "Betty, I know you can do as well as Marjorie," Mom would say. She would proudly display the card and point to the vertical line of capital A's. "See, she got a perfect grade in every subject. You just need to work harder and you can make good grades too."

The only A's I regularly received were in conduct. I never got into trouble. Out of obedience, I studied more, but the report card didn't improve. No matter how well I prepared for exams, I panicked, froze, and forgot everything when the test was placed in my hands. I felt inferior to other kids in my class, and I convinced myself I was incapable of learning the way my mother expected.

I hated disappointing the people who cared about me, but I had to face the facts. There were some things I simply could not do. Anything that resembled a test of my intelligence resulted in failure, so I did my best to avoid those situations. Out of fear I retreated into a quiet world. I smiled and nodded as if I understood what people were telling me. I didn't want them to find out what I knew: that I was dumb.

My parents, to their credit, never punished me for poor academic progress. They monitored my homework and witnessed my disappointment when grades never reflected my hours of study. Even though I wasn't an achiever like their other children, they still showed they believed in me and loved me. Yet rewards for academic success were always dangled in front of me to motivate improvement. When I never met the requirements, Mother and Daddy felt they had to recognize my hard work in some way and they did so. To this day I appreciate their efforts to affirm me. I know now that most of the disapproval I felt came from myself.

For instance, when I was in sixth grade, my daddy gave me a present that I treasured. In high school he had received an award for his achievements in sports. It was a small gold basketball, which he put on a matching chain and placed around my neck. I felt honored that I had been chosen to receive it. I wore it everywhere. Then one day in physical education class, the chain broke and I lost it. It crushed me that my parents had trusted me with such a cherished possession, and I had let them down. When I faced my father with the news, he told me I shouldn't feel bad about it. His words, while gracious, didn't help much. My sorrow ran too deep to accept mercy.

The behavior pattern of my childhood continued into my early teens. I seldom got in trouble at home or at school. I was afraid to be disobedient to any authority and hated the thought of punishment. Nevertheless, my good intentions didn't always produce the desired results.

A few days after receiving my driver's license I was permitted to use the family car to pick up some friends and get a frosted root beer. Operating the car independent of adult supervision was cause to celebrate. Everything went well until I returned home. Our driveway steeply inclined into the garage. As I approached, my foot slipped off the brake pedal and hit the accelerator. I collided into the side of the garage and did significant damage.

Pete and Helen harassed me for two hours before Daddy came home. "Miss Goody Two-shoes is finally gonna get it!"

"Just wait until Daddy sees what you did."

"You won't get out of this one."

The moment his car pool let him out, Daddy saw the destruction. I watched from the house as he saw the mangled garage wall and stopped. Nervously I stepped out to meet my father and take my punishment. The entire family gathered around as I did my best to explain what had happened.

His inspection was over within a few moments. Without looking up, he responded in his usual steady voice, "Honey, that's okay. That garage needed rebuilding anyway."

My brother and sisters were stunned. All evening I got looks that could kill and complaints of unfairness. What could I say? I didn't understand the mercy I had been shown, but I didn't question it. I just assumed it had something to do with being good.

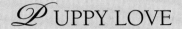UPPY LOVE

"THERE'S A REAL CUTE GUY LIVING WITH THE PASTOR AND HIS family this summer," my close friend said. "Promise me you'll stay away from him." She firmly planted her fists on her hips as her eyes narrowed in serious warning.

I was speechless. Why would she consider *me* a threat? "Don't worry," I assured her. "I just broke up with one boyfriend, and I'm not looking for another. You can have him."

My friend persisted. "I met this guy the other day, and I remember seeing him last summer when he visited Pastor Hale. I really want to date him."

"You're my best friend. I won't interfere. I promise."

Finally she heard the sincerity in my voice, and her shoulders heaved a frustrated sigh. She paused, folded her arms, and looked me right in the eyes. "Well, I know what will happen. He'll end up liking you."

Sunday morning at church I saw the guy she had

warned me about. I hadn't expected him to be so good-looking. I moved closer so I could study him. He was tall and thin, and his dark tan was a stark contrast to the white T-shirt he wore with his blue jeans. His smile was gentle and almost shy; he had a strong jaw and high cheekbones. When he turned and faced my direction, I looked into piercing dark eyes, the color of his jet-black hair.

Hmmm, he is cute. Maybe I made a mistake telling my good friend I had no interest in him. Then conviction stopped my traitorous thoughts. *No . . . I gave her my word.*

We had never competed for a boy's attention. At the age of fourteen, most of our social life was confined to our church youth group. My parents allowed me to date and "go steady," as we called it, if Mom approved of the young man. Dating consisted of getting a frosted root beer or stopping for a burger after church on Sunday and Wednesday nights. A date with a boy close to my age who regularly attended church generally brought her approval, but I always got her permission for the time and place.

In the Sunday night service, I noticed this cute guy, my friend's heartthrob, staring at me. I smiled, then looked away casually. I was told that his name was James. Curiosity kept my thoughts on him as I glanced his direction again. He was still looking at me.

Where was I when he visited last summer? Maybe our family was camping. I know I would have remembered him.

Someone said that Pastor and Mrs. Hale raised him

from infancy to age five, and then his mother took him back for ten years. I knew he wasn't the first boy who had been given a home with our pastor and his wife. In addition to their own daughter, Mary Doyle, they had raised Clayton Spriggs, a kind, young man, who was quite a bit older than me.

A story describing James' visit last summer had circulated among the youth. On the last Sunday evening of his visit, Mrs. Hale went before each Bible study class and requested prayer for God to save James before he returned home. That night the youth voluntarily stood and shared testimonies about Jesus' love. During the closing hymn, Mrs. Hale left her seat near the front to find James where he sat on the back pew. After they talked briefly, they walked to the front together. James told Brother Hale that he wanted to have what the teenagers had talked about. Everyone rejoiced that James had become a Christian.

Now, a year later, the Hales reintroduced James Robison to the congregation of Memorial Baptist Church. They asked the church family to make their fifteen-year-old foster son feel welcome as he attended the services with them each week until school started again in the fall. I listened to their request and thought to myself, *We could be seeing a lot of this guy in the summer months ahead.*

I had completed the ninth grade and was looking forward to a long summer vacation. Other than band and sports, school was a stressful place for me. I still faced the grueling task of completing grades ten through twelve, but I decided not to think about that. With no boyfriend and no homework for three months, I would throw myself into church activities. I knew the youth pastor depended on me and a few other teenagers to help him plan outreaches and fellowships.

Summer vacations were always busy and filled with fun. I wondered if James would want to participate. I planned to do just as my pastor and his wife asked— make him feel welcome. *That shouldn't cause any problems with my friend.*

Vacation Bible School, commonly called VBS, was our first event of the summer. Our church planned a full week of fun and learning centered on a Bible curriculum for children. Weeks in advance adults and teenagers promoted VBS to the community, increasing the numbers of preschool and elementary-age children who would attend.

The first day was wild. High-pitched voices roared through the hallways of the church as excited kids searched for their classrooms. The youth helpers eased the frenzy, guiding children to their assigned age-groups, then assisting teachers with the creative games, art, and music—all used to tell Bible stories and convey God's truths.

That morning I looked for James' tall frame each time we moved the kids through the corridors. I had been introduced to him after church on Sunday night and assumed he would be helping Mrs. Hale with her responsibilities, just as I was helping my mother with her class. At the scheduled time each age-group participated in outdoor recreation and refreshments supervised by the youth helpers. I located James when we went outside for games. He spoke to me, and later I noticed him watching me as we moved children toward the refreshment tables in the fellowship hall.

After punch and cookies were served, we cleaned the hall's many spills. The adult workers set aside generous portions of cookies with larger cups of punch. When our break was granted, we grabbed the cookies and escaped to the only place where children would not be found, the pastor's study. Brother Hale was busy closing the group session of VBS, so he was not aware of the invasion.

There were five of us the first day, and we felt it was okay to make ourselves comfortable. James seated himself in the chair behind the pastor's desk. He announced his role as president, appointed each of us parts to play, and an improvised executive-office game began. He asked me to be his personal secretary. I could tell he was flirting with me; the "president" kept his "secretary" near his desk and made frequent eye contact. I felt a little guilty because of my words to "you know who," but I really enjoyed his attention. And it helped that she wasn't in the room. She had talked with James several times before and after church, but it seemed obvious he wasn't interested in her. I was the only girl in our group getting his attention. I had not pursued him, but I made sure I stayed close enough to get "caught" when he approached me.

At the end of the first day, my mother found out we'd gone into the church offices when our work was finished. That was not acceptable behavior for her daughter, so I was told to walk home and prepare lunch. We lived only a few blocks away, but James asked if he could give me a ride. Mom gave her permission, and he drove me to my house in the Hales' station wagon.

On Wednesday James asked if we could go out after church. I already felt a strong attraction to him. The thought of a real date and an opportunity to be alone with him thrilled me. We visited the Grove, a popular drive-in restaurant where my friends hung out. I felt proud to be seen with James. Afterward he took a wrong turn and ended up in an empty parking lot behind an elementary school.

"Where are you taking me?" I asked suspiciously.

"Oh, I thought this was the way to your house," he explained as he stopped the car. "Would you mind if we stayed here a little while and talked?"

I wasn't sure he was telling the truth, but I agreed to sit and talk. We had a wonderful time laughing and getting to know each other. When he took me home, he stopped the car in front of my house and said good night.

I was a little puzzled as I let myself out of the car. *Why did he just drop me off at the curb? My dates always walk me to the door.*

Later Mrs. Hale told me that James had never dated before. She confessed that she quizzed him about his gentlemanly behavior when he returned that night. When he discovered how many mistakes he had committed on his first time out with me, he wanted to die.

"The first day in church, I was watching Betty, but she didn't know it," he confessed to Mrs. Hale. "When she turned and looked at me, she smiled. And, well, those dimples and her cute figure got me. Of all the girls I've met at church, she is the only one I want to date. She's the purest, sweetest girl in the world. Do you think she'll ever go out with me again?"

Mrs. Hale let him know she approved of the relationship and coached him in dating etiquette. In the weeks that followed she and Brother Hale loaned their car to James for more opportunities to get to know me.

From that point on he considered me his girlfriend. We were always together. I tried to explain to my friend how things had gone beyond my control, but it turned out she was right. I *was* a big threat to her, and James ended up liking me just as she had predicted. She refused to speak to me after that. It was sad to lose her friendship, but I gained a new companion who thought I was pretty and wanted to be with me every day.

"Doesn't James have something he needs to do?" Mom would sometimes ask. "He's over here all the time." While I was busy with ironing and other chores, he would sit nearby and talk. I loved his intelligent, creative personality. When adults described our relationship as "puppy love," James would make a comical reply. "Well, it's real to the dogs." His words and actions made me feel treasured, and I dreaded the thought of his leaving at the end of the summer.

Our three-month vacation was almost over when James announced to the Hales that he didn't want to go back home with his mother in Austin, Texas. He felt God wanted him to stay in Pasadena. Everyone supported his decision but knew it would be difficult for him to leave his mother alone. When the day came for his return to Austin, he asked his best friend, Larry Wilson, to go with him to collect his few personal things and help him tell his mother his decision. Larry had a way of keeping things lighthearted. Most important, he would give James the support he needed to actually make the break.

Through the summertime I had collected enough comments and stories from the Hales to be aware of the difficult life James faced during the ten years he lived with his mother, Myra. She had conceived him at the age of forty, after being raped. Her attacker was the alcoholic son of an elderly man she cared for as a live-in nurse. When she discovered she was pregnant, she attempted to get an abortion. But the doctor refused and encouraged her to have the baby.

When James was born, Myra was afraid she couldn't care for him, so she put an ad in the paper, asking someone to take him. Mrs. Hale answered the ad and brought the baby boy into their home while her husband was out of town. James was in very poor health as a newborn, and the doctors gave discouraging reports regarding his future. But the Hales nurtured him, and the church members joined them in praying for this baby to get well. In their care he grew strong and healthy. They were the only parents he knew until Myra reappeared to claim him five years later.

Losing James broke the Hales' hearts. They were worried about Myra's emotional instability and could only imagine the desperate poverty and possible neglect the little boy—whom they had come to think of as their own—was experiencing. They offered her financial support, but she refused their help. They wrote letters and sent gifts for James' birthday and Christmas, but all were returned. Myra made it clear she would never release her son into their custody again.

Amazingly James grew to love his mother very deeply in spite of what she had done. He never became bitter at her or the Hales. But he was grievously hurt when he didn't hear from the Hales for so many years. Eventually he assumed they had forgotten him. He had no idea that his mother intercepted the mail and sent the Hales' many letters and gifts back immediately. She believed she had to shut them out of her son's life in order to gain his love.

Myra lived in poverty, moved frequently, and then married a man named Sam, who couldn't read or write. Although he was a kind man, he couldn't provide for them, so the marriage didn't last very long. When James was very young, his mother left him with relatives for short periods, and he wondered if she would ever return. Eventually she would collect him and move into a one-room or two-room apartment behind a run-down house, or a shack in a slum area near the river.

The breaking point came when James reached his teens. Joe Robison, the abusive alcoholic who had raped James' mother and fathered him, suddenly reentered their lives. Myra announced to her son that she had married Joe so James would have his real father in his life.

The prospect of having a daddy and becoming a real family gave James hope until his drunken father staggered

33

into their yard the first day Joe came to live with them. James' dreams of tossing a ball back and forth in a game of catch disappeared as Joe lay drunk for days. When he was sober, he was abusive and stole from them to satisfy his thirst for alcohol. He robbed James of his life savings—a sum of thirteen dollars. If Joe couldn't get his hands on money, he would resort to drinking his hair tonic and other household liquids that contained alcohol.

On several occasions James and his mother experienced the effects of Joe's violent drunken attacks. One night James found his mother weeping and holding her throat. She described how his father had choked her until she passed out. She believed he would have killed her if she hadn't lost consciousness.

A few days later James was in the house alone when Joe Robison stumbled in through the front door, drunk and cursing. As he dropped heavily into a chair, he shouted, "I'm going to kill you, boy." James hurried to the closet in their other room, grabbed a 30.06 rifle, and loaded it with shells. He was shaking as he raised the rifle and aimed it at close range. His father continued cursing and yelling his threats as James carefully sat in the chair beside the phone. With the gun awkwardly positioned in one hand, ready to fire, his other hand dialed the operator to bring the police. Joe was much bigger than James, so pulling the trigger would have been necessary if his father had tried to overpower him. Miraculously the deputy sheriff appeared at the door and rescued James . . . or he possibly would have had to live the rest of his life with the heavy burden of guilt for killing his father.

That event led his mother to allow James a phone call to the Hales. James wasn't sure they would want to see him with no contact for ten years, but he had to try. His first visit to the Hales' home reassured him of their devoted love and revealed his mother's selfish effort to capture his affection. Now after two summer visits with Mom and Pop Hale, he was making it his permanent home.

I watched James and Larry board the Greyhound bus for Austin, and I hoped his mother would not change his mind. I prayed continuously from the time they left until the Hales and I arrived to pick him up in Austin two days later.

James wanted to serve God and grow in his Christian life. He realized that was not going to happen if he lived with his mother. And then there was me. Although James and I were young, we believed God had brought us together. I couldn't bear the thought of our ever being apart.

$\mathcal{P}$ASADENA HIGH

WHEN I ARRIVED IN AUSTIN, TEXAS, WITH PASTOR AND MRS. HALE, James and Larry were packed and waiting. We all felt sad for his mother, who had such a difficult life, but we were confident it was God's will for James to return to Pasadena. We loaded the car with his things, and I sat close to him in the backseat, so relieved that we would be able to continue our relationship because he *was* moving to Pasadena.

James enrolled in Pasadena High School as a junior, a grade ahead of me. We met each morning at school long before the first bell rang. I always arrived before James, because I hated ever being late. We talked until it was time to go to class and looked for each other throughout the day, snatching a quick minute between classes.

I played clarinet in the marching band, and he made the football team. I admired his confidence and determination in athletics, and he excelled scholastically with very little effort on homework. However, he was extremely shy about speaking before the class. He would take a zero on an assignment if it required an oral report. I didn't like speaking in front of people either, but I was more afraid not to obey when given an assignment.

Over the next two years our differences became most apparent in church activities. I loved singing in youth choir and attended all the youth events. James had trouble singing on pitch, so he didn't care for choir. He attended some youth functions just to be with me but never became regularly involved. I had close friends and was torn between spending time with them or with James. Once we broke up because I chose to go on a church hayride with the youth instead of a date alone with him. The next day after choir practice, he called me over to the car. We worked out our differences and got back together.

In early summer, after he graduated, I figured out a way to get him more interested in the youth group. Every year we planned a revival led entirely by young people. The guest preacher would be a dynamic, sixteen-year-old evangelist named Daniel Vestel. We customarily elected the other leadership positions, so I persuaded all my friends to nominate James for youth pastor. Of course he won. He realized I was responsible for the nomination unanimously falling to him and was angry when he heard the job description, because he was so shy. For one week he would sit on the platform each night and introduce Daniel. During the day James was to be Daniel's personal companion and driver for any ministry appointments he might have.

Within a few days, it was obvious that Daniel Vestel was being used by God to influence James. Everywhere they went Daniel talked about the Word of God, quoting more Scripture than James thought a human mind could hold. Each evening Daniel demonstrated how a young man could preach powerful messages.

On the Friday night of the revival I sat in the youth choir, as usual. Daniel preached an inspiring message, and the choir stood to sing a song of commitment. I watched James leave his seat and go to Brother Hale. They talked for a few moments and then prayed together. When the music stopped, Brother Hale spoke with a father's emotion as he shared James' decision with the congregation. "James feels that God has called him to be an evangelist."

My heart nearly stopped as I realized the Lord really *had* spoken to James. And, as a result, James committed his whole life to the ministry. I saw shocked expressions on the faces of youth and adults seated in the pews. Mrs. Hale leaped up and became so excited I was afraid she would have a heart attack. Brother Hale's eyes filled with joyful tears as he embraced his foster son.

From that night on, James' life was transformed. He possessed an inner confidence and drive I'd never seen before. His insatiable appetite for God's Word caused every date to be an evening of memorizing Scripture together. His timidity in speaking was replaced by a desire to boldly share the gospel with everyone. I could tell he was nervous, but it was like he couldn't hold it back.

Monday after the youth revival he was back at his construction job at Petro-Tex Chemical Plant. During lunch he jumped onto a flatbed truck in an open yard filled with construction workers. "Listen!" James shouted. "I'm just a young teenage boy trying to learn how to be a man." The sudden appearance of a tall, muscular eighteen-year-old demanded the attention of redneck tough guys stuffing down bologna sandwiches. "I wouldn't talk about a dog the way some of you talk about your wives." All eyes remained fixed on him as he told how he had come to love Jesus and that Jesus loved them too. His message was brief but effective. A few heads even dropped in conviction; no one made wisecracks.

When the lunch hour ended, they all returned to their duties. There seemed to be less chatter than usual. Then it started. "Helper," men would yell in the customary way of summoning James, "would you give me a hand?" Invariably these men sought more than help with their jobs. In brokenness they would ask James to tell them more. In the three days following his first outdoor sermon, four men accepted Jesus as their Savior.

The rest of the summer James developed a deep intimacy with God. At one point he said, "Betty, Jesus has become as real to me as you are." He related how he spent time talking and listening to the Lord. He was always eager to share with me and report what God was showing him.

He left in the fall for East Texas Baptist University. On many afternoons after school I received his letters, filled with praises to the Lord. He described a special place in the woods where he daily went to pray. Of course he wrote his love expressions for me as well, but the majority of his letters detailed his passion for Jesus.

The exciting events that followed James' call into evangelism stirred in me a confusing mixture of thoughts and emotions. I'd heard about Jesus all my life, but he was not as real to me as he was to James.

I remembered back to when I was ten years old and our church held a special revival led by a husband-and-wife team. The wife of the evangelist met each night with the children; then all the church came together to hear the husband preach. In the adult service children were pressured to come to the front and make a decision. Pete and Marjorie had made decisions a year or so before that revival. They had joined the church and were baptized. Even Helen had gone forward earlier that week during the revival. I was the only one who hadn't made a commitment.

Toward the end of the week, when the evangelist's wife coaxed the children again, I fearfully stepped out. The lady's words scared me. I didn't want to go to hell, so I made a decision. But no one talked to me at that time about asking Jesus to forgive my sins or be my Savior. Instead they had me sign a card and sit down on the front pew. *Now I am like everyone else*, I thought.

Later, as I read James' letters, I reflected upon my years of church work and realized that fear had motivated my service to God. I thought he would punish me if I didn't dutifully obey his commandments. I loved God but had trouble comprehending the love relationship

41

James was experiencing where there was an intimate, two-way communication.

One night James and I attended a Saturday night service at another church where a great singer, Jerry Wayne Bernard, ministered. His music touched my heart, and once again I heard a passionate testimony about real intimacy with Jesus. I compared my relationship with what the singer had described.

42

On the drive home the confusion about my salvation increased to heavy conviction. It was difficult for me to share my thoughts with James as I fought to suppress my emotions, but I finally got the words out: "James, I don't know if I'm saved." He patiently opened his Bible and read aloud the underlined Scriptures for salvation. I listened to the words I had memorized years before to meet the requirements for witnessing on Thursday night visitation. I wondered if all I possessed was a mental image of God and not a personal relationship from my heart.

James never told me what I needed to do but was sensitive to let me hear God for myself and leave the rest to the Holy Spirit. Before he left he assured me he would be praying for me.

That night I sat on the bathroom floor, reading the Scriptures and begging God for an answer. I was afraid if I went to bed, I would die in my sleep and miss heaven. I couldn't feel anything but torment and confusion.

What would people think if they knew I had never really been saved? It would be so embarrassing to walk in front of all the people who knew me and confess that I was a lost church member. What had I been doing all these years—

going to church four and five times a week, teaching Sunday school, reading my Bible, and praying faithfully? What good had it done me?

Some of the phrases from the Scriptures James had read came to my mind. *"Not of works, lest anyone should boast."*

I started with the preceding verse from memory: *"For by grace you have been saved through faith . . . not of works, lest anyone should boast."* I had been seeking God and trying to please him with my works as long as I could remember.

"I am the way, the truth, and the life. No one comes to the Father except through me."

That says it pretty clearly, I admitted. *I have to accept Jesus' sacrifice for my sins to be forgiven. My sins . . . I've worked very hard not to sin—ever. I've tried to be a righteous person.*

"Our righteousnesses are like filthy rags!"

Next to Jesus, I thought, *I fail the righteousness test. I'm a sinner, and I need to confess him before men or he will never confess me before my heavenly Father.*

"Help me, Lord. I'm afraid to close my eyes. I want to find your peace," I cried aloud. "Please don't leave me! You know I will obey you—whatever you tell me to do. I always have."

The next morning was Sunday, and I assumed my usual routine. I taught my Sunday school class of young girls, sang in the choir, and even sang a duet with my sister for the special music before the pastor's message. When the invitation hymn started, I quickly left my

43

conspicuous spot in the choir to kneel and pray at the front of the auditorium. I prayed until God's peace came, and then I approached Brother Hale to share my decision. He gently reached for me and leaned in to hear my words.

"I just got saved over there," I stated confidently. I watched his shocked reaction; for a few moments he was speechless.

"What? Why, Betty, you are the best girl in our church!"

"Brother Hale, I am tired of hearing about how good I am. I'm tired of trying to be what I'm not! I needed Jesus to save me. I prayed and asked him, and he did it."

James rejoiced with me after the service. Suddenly it occurred to me how important it would be for the wife of an evangelist to have a personal relationship with Jesus Christ. Now I understood James' passion for the Lord. At last I felt God's love for me and knew I did not have to earn his favor. The sweetness of my fellowship with my Lord was precious; I praised him and told him I loved him. My new relationship was so fulfilling; God felt near to me.

I had no idea how much I would need him for all the lonely days ahead.

*T*OGETHER

Mr. and Mrs. Victor Freeman request
the honor of your presence
at the marriage of their daughter
Betty Catherine
to
Evangelist James Robison
on Saturday, the twenty-third of February
nineteen hundred and sixty-three
at half past seven o'clock
Memorial Baptist Church
323 South Main
Pasadena, Texas

THE MOMENT I'D BEEN WAITING FOR CAME MY SENIOR YEAR OF high school: James gave me an engagement ring. The small round diamond looked as big as James' heart, and I proudly showed it to all my friends. Being married and caring for a family was the fulfillment of all my career goals.

With no desire for college, as soon as I graduated from high school I got a job as a mail clerk and a telephone operator for an industrial supply company. Most of my paycheck went into our wedding savings account. James and I assumed that responsibility because my parents couldn't afford the expense at that time.

The money James deposited came from the small love offerings he received for preaching revivals. He partnered with Billy Foote, a fellow theology student and talented singer from East Texas Baptist University. Billy had an outgoing, comical personality, and his enthusiasm for ministry equaled James'. Because Billy believed James had a special gift from God, he agreed to lead the music and sing solos for any church meetings they could get.

From the reports of the large numbers of people coming to know Christ, most people thought Billy and James' success had come overnight. However, I knew how difficult it had been to secure meetings, especially in the beginning. James and Billy had visited many Baptist churches in east and southeast Texas, sharing an exciting vision for evangelizing their community. Even though most pastors wouldn't even take the time to listen to them, the two young men kept trying. Eventually a few pastors saw the heart and passion of the dynamic duo and scheduled a weekend meeting. Each revival inspired the congregation to share their faith, and many came to know Jesus.

Throughout all of this ministry, James was carrying a full load of classes each semester. And yet he did well, even with the tiring weekend travel. Referrals and praise reports spread from churches where they had been. In the next year Billy and James received a thousand invitations. The Lord impressed them to take a six-month break from school so they could schedule more revivals.

The meetings kept James and Billy on the road, and I traveled to join them whenever the church wasn't too far and my parents approved. I studied my fiancé as he preached. He had become so dynamic in the pulpit, I could barely remember the shy young man who couldn't give a report to his high school classmates. Each night God gave him boldness to stand before a large crowd of strangers, and he preached the gospel with great authority.

James was determined to communicate his message in the most effective way, so he practiced his gestures before a mirror. Certain movements seemed to accentuate his words, so he coordinated the motion of his arms and hands in the rhythm with his statements while carefully guarding against distracting actions.

I was proud of James and marveled at how God was blessing his ministry. All I could think of was becoming his wife. The date of our wedding moved three times, and each change cut weeks from our wait.

As the plans came together, we were amazed how God's provision erased major expenses from our strained budget. Beautiful bouquets and floral arrangements were designed in the shop owned by Pastor and Mrs. Hale's daughter, Mary Doyle, and her husband, Melvin. Mrs. Hale gave her daughter creative assistance, and they presented the wedding flowers as a gift to us. My mother

47

worked for a bakery at the time, and her employer donated a large three-layer cake for our reception. Mom added her special touch to the decorating. And that wasn't all. My mother's precise alterations on the borrowed bridal gown made the velveteen-and-lace, princess-style dress fit perfectly. A pearl-beaded, short veil draped lightly over the high lace at my neck. The long sleeves, tapered with tiny buttons to a point on my wrists, and the full hoop skirt made me feel so feminine.

I chose modest shrimp-colored dresses for my attendants. My two sisters were bridesmaids, and Winky Stark, Billy Foote's fiancée, was my maid of honor. Winky and I had become good friends as we followed our guys to their revival meetings. When I visited James at college, she let me share her room.

All preparations that required money went smoothly. However, one other detail brought our plans to a standstill. In the sixties, Texas law required a groom under the age of twenty-one to obtain a parent's signature granting permission to marry. James asked Myra, his mother, to sign for him, but she refused. The Hales had never obtained legal custody of James, so consent had to be secured from James' biological father. Many phone calls and inquiries finally led us to Joe Robison's new residence, a California prison. We knew Joe's sister, Aunt Berta, lived in California, so we asked her to get the signature for us. There was no speedy way of handling the legal paperwork. Everything was done by mail, and delivery was very slow.

The day before the wedding, the letter still had not

arrived. The stress and uncertainty forced me to make a decision, which I announced to James with unusual boldness: "We will go through with this wedding—with or without the signature. After the ceremony is over, we will split up and go our separate ways. When we have your father's signature, we can get married legally. Only then will we go on our honeymoon."

James agreed. He could see in my eyes that it would be no other way. I'm sure, because of his intense prayers, the signed document came just in time for our honeymoon not to be delayed. I prayed some pretty desperate prayers myself.

February 23, our wedding day, finally arrived, complete with heavy thunderstorms. I was happy the rain stopped by the time we unloaded my personal things to finish dressing at the church. My hair had been beautifully styled at the beauty shop that morning, but the damage from the humidity greeted me in the mirror as we attempted to put on my veil.

"I hate my hair," I said as Mom fussed with the fabric, shaping and fluffing it to disguise what was under it.

Finally she stepped back with a verdict I already knew. "Honey, your hair has been teased and sprayed heavily, and that awful, wet air has pasted it down like plaster. As straight as your hair is, you'd lose what little curl you have left if you tried to brush it or rearrange it."

We positioned the veil as best we could to camouflage my limp curls, then took inventory of the traditional items required: something old, something new, something borrowed, and something blue.

"Okay, I'm ready," I said, with an intake of breath.

As soon as the entrance to the sanctuary closed, my attendants and I met my father in the back of the church. I heard the wedding march begin, the doors opened, and my heart almost burst with excitement. When I looked to the front of the church, I forgot all about the weather and my limp hair. James, so handsome in his white jacket, black pants, and black bow tie, was staring at me. I couldn't suppress the wide smile on my face. He was waiting for me to come to him.

On the musical cue the flower girl stepped out, dropping tiny petals several feet ahead of me. Next came my three attendants—my two sisters and Winky, Billy Foote's girlfriend, soon to be his fiancée.

Then all eyes turned toward the aisle when I made my entrance. Surprisingly, I wasn't nervous at all! I was happy to see that the rain hadn't kept our school friends and church family away. And I couldn't contain my joy even though I sensed my father's nervousness as we walked arm in arm down the aisle.

When Brother Hale asked, "Who gives this bride?" Daddy was supposed to say, "Her mother and I do." But he didn't answer. When the question was repeated, again with no response, I nudged him in his side with my elbow. After a few seconds he timidly answered, "I do." As I looked into his eyes, tears filled mine. I was really touched by his emotional expression of love. Then Daddy stepped back to join Mom on the second pew, and James slipped into his spot beside me.

James nervously took my arm. I squeezed his fingers

to calm him as our hands joined for the vows. Billy stood on the other side of James as his best man, and when we knelt to pray, Billy knelt beside James. For me that was the most touching moment in the ceremony.

The wedding wasn't long, and our reception followed in the hall adjoining the church. As I tossed the bridal bouquet, we heard the rain begin again. We would be running through more than rice to reach the getaway vehicle that would take us to our car's hiding place. My going-away suit, hat, and gloves were drenched by the time we made the final connection and were alone in our car.

We escaped in the used Corvair James and I had purchased together during our engagement. On the thirty-minute drive to our honeymoon spot in Galveston the storm pounded our car. Visibility was poor, and the slick street sent us into three full spins and a near miss with an oncoming car. We were still shaking long after the car stopped its revolving.

Once in Galveston, we called the Hales and described the danger we had faced. Everyone thanked God our lives had been protected. At our honeymoon spot, James picked me up in his arms and shoved open the motel-room door. "Wait a minute," he said, still holding me as he looked around. "There's no bed in this room!" He put me down and dialed the front desk. "Hey, we are on our honeymoon, and we want a real bed." The manager informed us there were no other rooms available and explained how to convert the two sofas into beds. That was not James' idea of a honeymoon bed, so he converted them and then shoved them together. Our romantic first night was at last under way . . . or so we thought.

We were into a passionate embrace when we heard someone put a key into our lock. James leaped to the door, body-slamming it shut just in time. "This room is already taken," he yelled, "and we are on our honeymoon!"

When James called the desk to report the problem, we learned they had accidentally assigned someone to our room. James reminded them this was our wedding night, and we did not want to be disturbed. After sincere apologies, the desk clerk assured us our privacy would be guarded.

We had only one night and one day in Galveston. Even if my employer had given me more time from work, we couldn't afford the Gulf-beach accommodations. When James checked us into the motel, we had thirty dollars. After settling our bill, he climbed into the driver's seat with a downcast expression. There was only enough left to have lunch before we went home.

We drove to a clear, open section of the coast, put on our heavy coats, and took a long walk on the windy beach. Wintry, gray ocean waves washed the storm's debris upon the sand as we strolled near the seawall. We talked about our future, and the budget we knew we would have to maintain in the months ahead. James paused to pray, thanking God in advance for the way he would meet our needs.

Then we found a café with a view of the Texas Gulf and shared our last honeymoon meal.

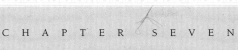JUST ORDINARY

WHEN JAMES AND I HAD BEEN MARRIED FOR A MONTH, WE moved into a fully furnished, rent-free house owned by friends of the Hales who needed house sitters for six months. The opportunity to move from our tiny one-bedroom apartment to a two-bedroom house, with no expenses, was a great relief with our small income.

I stared at myself in the bathroom mirror. It had been only half an hour since James drove away for a revival in Texarkana. I was alone again. The house was a blessed place when James and I were there together, but it became a prison when he was gone.

Fearful thoughts had begun to trouble me daily, even when James and I were together. But my mind was more tormented when he left on trips. *He'll be gone for days. What am I going to do during this time without him?* I knew James wouldn't be alone; he'd be surrounded day and night by people who loved and appreciated him. I had been to enough of his ministry meetings to visualize the special attention he would receive. Even more, I knew that many of the people around him could be women who found him attractive. After all, his powerful gift drew large crowds. Each night many responded, turning their lives completely to the Lord.

Even though James always assured me of his love and complete devotion to me, I began to battle within my own heart. My insecurity grew—I felt that I wasn't pretty or smart enough or gifted enough to be his wife.

These struggles had been locked up inside me for a long, long time and were just coming to the surface. Today I'm convinced that as God was so mightily using James to touch and change lives, the enemy knew he had to try to lessen that dynamic effect.

We were so in love as newlyweds that I spent most of my time thinking about how much I loved James and wanted to be the perfect wife. But because I was so insecure, I just couldn't accept that I could be everything he wanted and needed. So I helped Satan out by putting myself down all the time.

James continued to compliment and encourage me. But I would usually throw it right back in his face, so to speak, by telling him all the reasons I didn't think anything he said about me was true. I allowed Satan to paint pictures in my mind, even though James had never given me any reason to entertain such thoughts. Satan would take the fact that James loved and cared about people, no matter who they were, and twist that completely innocent heart for God and plant doubt in my mind. I knew women saw his strength and leadership as godly attributes, not to mention the fact that James was handsome too.

All of those thoughts condemned me as I looked in the mirror and glared at the person I thought was such a disappointment to everyone. I just knew there were many girls and women who hungered for a close relationship with a strong man who had a love for God.

James is everything they have dreamed of, I would think. *How did I get him? I'm so ordinary. The mirror doesn't lie.*

One day I lifted the limp strands of hair covering my ears and angled my face to the side, profiling my short, turned-up nose. I never liked my pug nose. Why couldn't it contour gradually and be a little longer? I hated my long jaw—it made my chin jut out too far. If only I had high, prominent cheekbones, my face would be better proportioned.

After a close examination I dropped my hair back down where it touched near my shoulders, hiding my ears and hopefully disguising my long neck. *Maybe I should change my hair color to blonde or dark brown or try a perm,* I told myself. *Anything but plain, mousy brown that never holds curl.*

If James could have heard my thoughts, he would have been concerned—especially since he had often pleaded with me to see myself the way he did. He regularly complimented my looks and, like my grandfather, made a big deal over my smile. He would caress my face and plant kisses on the dimples in my cheeks.

Discouraged by my image, I turned off the bathroom light and walked into our bedroom, where the sight of myself in the dresser mirror stopped me again. *James doesn't see my outward appearance realistically,* I thought. *There is nothing special about me.*

In contrast, there was nothing ordinary about James. He deserved someone with beauty and talent. I didn't have the gifts that the wife of a great evangelist was supposed to have. I knew what people were thinking when James introduced me at his revival meetings. They might as well have said it out loud. "She is so plain. I really expected James to have a more glamorous wife." After the service, the women near my seat would greet me and try to make conversation, but I never made it easy for them. I was afraid they would ask a question I couldn't answer. I smiled and spoke—perhaps one full sentence. By making minimal eye contact, I tried not to encourage more conversation that led to questions like "Do you sing, Betty? play the piano or teach Bible studies?"

"No, I don't do anything special," I wanted to scream. "James got the wrong wife, don't you agree?" I had taken piano lessons, but I didn't play well. I could sing, but I felt I had an ordinary voice. Singing harmony was my preference so I'd never have to sing solo. I didn't feel qualified to teach the Bible because I sometimes had trouble comprehending what I read and depended on James to help me understand.

When I traveled to James' meetings to be with him, I begged not to be introduced to the congregation. But

James would say encouragingly, "Honey, I'm proud of you, and I want people to meet you." Some nights I didn't attend, simply to avoid the attention. If I went, I sat near the back, hoping to make it difficult for people to spot me. When he insisted on a public introduction, I stood up before the glaring eyes of the crowd long enough to appease him, then quickly sat down.

Before long, I knew that James was growing more exasperated with me, whether I went to a meeting or stayed home. When he had a few days home, I refused to accept an invitation where I would have to share him with someone. Tense conversations resulted, and he accused me of possessiveness. I excused my actions with my most sincere belief: "James, the problem is you don't love me as much as I love you. I don't need other people around. I just want to be with you."

I even resented the time James spent maintaining his intimate relationship with Jesus. Envious, pessimistic thoughts distorted my relationship with God, making me believe I was incapable of entering the depth of relationship James had. I thought it was only for special people, like church leaders. My husband's devotion to spiritual things forced my emotions into a taunting world of jealousy. *God has more of his time than you do, Betty. How can you compete with God?*

The problems in our relationship escalated. "You make me not want to come home," James shouted one day, at his wit's end. "I call you every day when I am away, and all you do is describe how miserable you are because I am not here. Then when I do come home, you act depressed and won't do anything or go anywhere. I don't know what to do." He walked out the front door.

I cried hysterically, "Don't you leave me," as I watched him drive away. I ran to the kitchen and pulled a butcher knife from the drawer. *I might as well kill myself so he can be rid of me. Then he can get the wife he needs,* I thought in agony. But I couldn't go through with it. As I returned the knife to the drawer, I belittled myself for lacking even the courage to end my life. For hours I sat alone with my fearful, ragged emotions, feeling guilty for entertaining the thought of suicide. What was wrong with me, anyway?

When James returned, he explained that he had left to control his anger and pray. I confessed how I had gotten the knife and wanted to kill myself. My drastic action obviously concerned and frightened him, and he searched for words to reassure me of his love as he held me in his arms.

That conflict exposed my jealousy and the potential seriousness of our early marital struggles. But since we didn't know how to stop my disturbing thought patterns that created the tension between us, we settled into a method of coping with my behavior.

James was such a transparent person, and the only way he knew to help me was to openly confront the problem. However, exposing my fears made me too vulnerable. I was afraid I would never be able to meet everyone's expectations. So I learned to pretend. I hid my fears and worked diligently to express myself in a way that kept people from pressing in to know me. People were still a threat, but I accepted the fact that James had the special touch of God, and I hoped there would be enough love left over for me. My needs would have to be adjusted in order to share him with God and others.

Then we learned I was pregnant, and the preparation for the birth of our first baby gave me a new focus during James' travel periods. I decided to quit work and become a full-time mom when I neared the delivery date. We were so excited about the coming birth. By now the retired couple who had so graciously allowed us to live in their house for six months had returned home, so we moved to a small one-bedroom apartment. On Wednesday afternoon, April 8, 1964, Rhonda was born. James was in a revival across town from the hospital and was expected to preach that night. After only a few minutes with his new daughter, he rushed to the church in the heavy evening traffic. I was told his sermon was the shortest he had ever preached.

Rhonda weighed 7 pounds, 12 ounces, and was 18½ inches long. I was glad she had James' black hair and olive complexion. Everyone thought she looked like her daddy, and I couldn't have been more pleased. When Rhonda and I were released from the hospital, we stayed with my parents for the week so I could have my mother's help.

Within days James had to leave again, this time to Dallas for a full week. It was so difficult for him to leave us. We talked each night while he was on the road, and I assured him I was doing well. I described everything about my day with Rhonda, but my words only made the ache of separation worse. We were so miserable apart. With my mother protesting, I got my doctor's permission and packed everything I would need to care for a ten-day-old infant and flew to Dallas. James was thrilled.

A short time after Rhonda was born, we moved to a two-bedroom, unfurnished apartment. Then, when Rhonda was eight months old, the Hales helped us purchase a small, ten-by-fifty-foot mobile home that had one and a half bedrooms. The half bedroom was just large enough for a baby bed. We were excited to have our own place, but we didn't own any furniture. A few purchases had to be added to our collection of donated pieces to make a home for our growing family.

A pattern developed—a flow of lifestyle that seemed to work for James and me as the calendar filled with invitations to preach. I devoted myself to making a perfect home, but achieving that goal was much easier for me when James was with me. When the weekend meetings became weeklong revivals, the separation became unbearable for the three of us. James had us join him during the middle of the week or on the weekend as often as our finances would allow. In those days churches were unable to assist much with the lodging and food for the evangelistic team, so the cost of housing and feeding your family on the road came from your own pocket.

Since Billy Foote had felt led by the Lord to take a position in a church as a music minister, James now teamed with John McKay. Older than Billy and more experienced in evangelistic ministry, John had the ability to enthusiastically lead the congregational singing and organize a large choir that sang special songs each night.

Rhonda began to show a talent for singing by the time she learned to talk well. She and I sang together a lot during our long drives to join James. She quickly learned the words and melodies to some of our favorite songs. We loved hearing the choir music. Singing congregational songs with the crowd was a treat for both of us.

By the time she was two, John brought her on stage to sing solos. I was so pleased to see her stand before large crowds, just as confident as her daddy. She communicated with the charm of her father's big dark eyes, and the crowd responded with spontaneous applause and loud amens. When she finished singing, James picked her up and kissed her. "You sang your song so well, Rhonda. I'm proud of you for using your voice to bless people. Are you afraid to sing in front of so many people?"

Her answer was always, "No, I not afraid."

After she sang for several meetings, however, we saw a change in her presentation when she was lifted to the stage. By the age of four or five she strutted onstage like a seasoned performer, grabbed the microphone from John, insisting she could hold it without his help. Our concern over her behavior made James tell her she would have to stop singing for a while. When asked by friends why she didn't sing solos anymore, she replied, "My daddy says I can't sing until I learn to be more shy."

John and his wife, Julia, had four children and lived in Fort Worth, Texas. Julia was an amazing woman, and

I sensed she really understood my loneliness. When we moved to Fort Worth, Rhonda and I leaned heavily on her strength and were welcomed into her crowded home for several days and nights while our husbands were ministering out of town.

I admired Julia's confidence and learned a lot about maintaining family life without James around. In a new community and church I needed encouragement to meet people and let Rhonda make friends her own age. Julia helped me adjust.

But I was not as fearless as Julia when household appliances or cars broke down. When repairs were needed, she simply made the decision and handled the situation, then told John what happened and how she took care of it. Too timid to call a repairman, I chose to put things off until James returned.

I grew more confident with making a perfect home. Being a good homemaker became the thing I felt most gifted to do. I loved ironing shirts and keeping the house clean while constantly attending to Rhonda's needs. Before long I was quite comfortable staying home while James was away. It seemed like the perfect time to have another baby.

$\mathcal{H}$IS WAY, HIS TIME

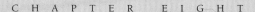

"JAMES, I HAVE THIS DEEP LONGING FOR ANOTHER CHILD."

The feeling had been building for some time, and I had to share it. Rhonda had brought great joy into our home, but she was becoming a very independent three-year-old who required less cuddling from me. Daily I dreamed of having another baby, and my heart's desire was for a son. James agreed, so we prayed and asked God to bless our family with another child.

In the months following, there seemed to be an epidemic of pregnancies among my friends. Even Julia McKay announced she was pregnant with her fifth child. I grew impatient and angry with God for overlooking me.

Then some female-related pain and discomfort sent me seeking a doctor's help. I learned that I had a tumor on my right ovary. The doctor's urgency in scheduling my surgery before I left his office really frightened James and me. Like most people who had lost friends and loved ones to cancer, we connected the word *tumor* with that dreaded, and often fatal, illness.

In the hospital, during my recovery, the doctor approached James with a serious expression and strained tone. "I want to talk with you about Betty's condition, but I think it needs to be with both of you. We'll talk when the anesthetic has completely worn off."

Fear gripped James. He rallied our friends to pray and had a sleepless night. Although he imagined the worst diagnosis, he never gave me any indication that there was a potential problem.

Several days passed. James thought, *Where is the doctor?* But he protected me from knowing of his concern. He knew I'd become very fearful. Yet he was certain it must be cancer. When the doctor finally visited my hospital room, he told us that the removal of my ovary had gone well, and the tumor was benign. A great weight lifted from James' shoulders but returned when he realized the doctor wasn't through with the prognosis.

The doctor paused, as if searching for the right words. "You have endometriosis." He described the condition that builds up scar tissue in the fallopian tubes and uterus. The problem was not life threatening, and a different gynecologist had already told us about it earlier. While we were relieved to hear a diagnosis we already knew, James was upset about the days of anxiety the doctor had put him through.

I started seeing a different physician in whom I had great confidence. Hoping for a favorable report on my condition and encouragement about another pregnancy,

I was disappointed. After examining me and conducting tests, the doctor said I had been fortunate to give birth to my first child. He speculated that the endometriosis had developed during my teens and worsened after my pregnancy. He encouraged James and me to enjoy our daughter and not to get our hopes up. The chances of conceiving a child with one functioning ovary and endometriosis would be slim to none.

In spite of the diagnosis James and I prayed that I would miraculously conceive. Month after month I begged God for a son, but my doctor's words were proving to be accurate. My barrenness affected me deeply when expectant friends gave birth. The torment of my envious, resentful thoughts and the anger I felt toward God controlled me. I was miserable with self-pity.

65

Then, step-by-step, the Lord began to break my heart over my attitude. I repented and begged him to take away the emptiness and the hunger for birthing another child. In the days following, I felt his forgiveness and peace, and finally found contentment in having Rhonda. I laid down the dream of giving birth to a son and resolved to care for the family and blessings God had given me.

One day, for no reason I could identify, I felt a strong desire to pursue adoption. I spoke with James and he said, "Betty, I love Rhonda so much. If we never have another child, I will be content. I'm traveling so much this decision needs to be yours. I'll support you, whatever you decide."

I wasn't used to making critical choices for our

family, but I knew he had spoken wisely. I sought the Lord and felt God wanted us to adopt a son. We spoke to a lawyer friend and filed the necessary papers.

And a miracle happened: Nine months to the day after God put adoption on my heart, a baby boy was born, and he would become our son.

I had returned from the grocery store one Saturday morning, August 30, 1969, when the call came. Mrs. Hale, or "Mimi," was there, caring for Rhonda.

"Betty, are you sitting down?" The lawyer sounded excited.

"Yes," I answered.

"Well, your son is here."

I shouted across the room, "Mimi, we've got a son."

"The birth mother reported that he was born a little premature, but the doctor said he was a healthy 6 pounds, 5 ounces. They will release him from the hospital Tuesday, and we'll pick him up. If you'd like, you can pick out a special outfit for him to wear home. Just get it to us, and we'll dress him and bring him to you."

"We get our baby boy on Tuesday!" I announced as soon as I hung up. Mimi, Rhonda, and I rejoiced together.

James had just started a citywide crusade in Tulsa, but I knew it was a good time to possibly reach him in his room.

"Hello." His voice sounded tired.

"James, you need to sit down." I wanted to create the anticipation I had experienced.

"What's going on?"

"You just need to sit down," I repeated.

"Okay, I'm sitting down. What is it?"

"James, your son is here."

He shouted so loud I had to hold the phone away from my ear.

"God is so good. He's answered our prayer," James said.

I gave him all the details about the baby's birth and how soon they would bring him to us. James wasn't scheduled to come home for five days and was sad that he would not be there to receive our baby into our family.

Three days wasn't much time to prepare for a baby in the house. I had bought a few things, but I still needed the most urgent items. There was no time for a baby shower, but many kind friends, who had heard the news, inquired about our needs and brought gifts. Mimi and I rushed into some frantic shopping for the remaining items, and the nursery came together just in time.

I purchased an adorable blue outfit that matched a tiny knit cap James had worn as a newborn. I sent that, along with a blanket and an infant carrier, to the hospital by way of the lawyer.

On a rainy Tuesday morning, a car pulled into our driveway. Our lawyer opened the car door and popped the umbrella to shelter his wife and the tiny bundle she was holding. They entered our house and immediately placed our little boy in my arms. I pulled back the edge of the receiving blanket. My beautiful son was sleeping peacefully. His skin was fair, and his hair reddish. When I touched his warm, velvety skin, he stirred and stretched, revealing very large hands for such a tiny body. His ears were the smallest I'd ever seen on a baby. I stroked them lovingly. Eventually he opened his big eyes to reveal the same blue-green as my eyes. He didn't cry, so I explored further, counting fingers and toes as I had done when Rhonda was born. Many feelings were the same as I remembered after giving birth. The most amazing was the overwhelming love for this little boy that poured from my heart.

I want to be the best mother for you. You're so beautiful. I hope your daddy is as taken with you as I am. I longed for James to be there, welcoming his son home. He was missing such a special moment. However, my time alone with our son provided the bonding I needed to feel. Once again I gained confidence in caring for a tiny baby.

During the quiet hours of the first evening's feedings, God gave me a greater understanding of the way he loves us. I wondered when I had Rhonda if I could love another child as much as I loved her. I had only begun to know our son, but I already felt the same measure of love for him. I realized I'd had a misconception about God's love—that he probably didn't love everyone the same. I'd believed he had favorites, people who received more love, mercy, and grace from him than others.

Now, as I stared at the gift I held in my arms, I knew differently. God is always adding to his family, and yet he has enough love to go around. I thanked him for showing me the truth about his love for us and smiled as my thoughts explored his greatness. *You make us feel like we're your only child.*

When James and I spoke finally by phone, I was gushing with emotion. "I can't wait for you to get home and hold him." I searched for words to describe what I had experienced when this special little boy was placed in my arms. "I know how much you love Rhonda, but I'm sure love for this little guy will overpower you too. Do you realize we would have missed this precious gift if God had answered my prayer and I had become pregnant last year?"

"You're right," James answered. "The Lord had a better plan. He knew this baby would need us to love him as our very own."

James and I both knew, without a doubt, that adoption was the right decision. And James expressed his eagerness to get acquainted with our new baby. "I'll be home as soon as I can," he said excitedly.

We named our little boy James Randall Robison, or Randy. Some people thought he favored me since his coloring was similar to mine. He was loved and received joyfully by everyone.

With the sudden growth of our family we made special efforts to help Rhonda feel loved. She was now a kindergartner, already having to adjust to school life after spending five years alone with me. She'd never had to compete for my attention. Now she came home each day and watched Mommy caring for a new baby brother.

One day, when I was feeding Randy a bottle, she pressed in close and asked, "Mommy, do you love me as much as you love him?"

I put my arm around her. "Honey, my love for you

is as great as it's always been. I love both of you." I knew she loved Randy but needed to hear there was still enough love for her. In the following months I would find her climbing into the playpen when she came home from school, just to be near her brother.

Rhonda became a great helper, and she and Randy grew very close. James adored his son and was amazed at how sweet he was. Randy was such a peaceful child and never gave us a moment's concern when it came to obedience. Later, as a toddler, he even put himself to bed when it was nap time. His personality was gentle and compliant. James commented one day, "You know, it's like this little guy knows he's special and that we chose him. You have to wonder if he is showing his gratitude by trying not to be any trouble."

Two years went by, with James and me enjoying our children, our home, and a blessed ministry. My prayer to birth another baby had been forgotten. Then I began to experience some discomfort. When I called the doctor's office, the nurse told me to come in, that I might be pregnant. I knew that wasn't likely, after everything I'd been through, but I wanted to find the cause of my pain. So I made an appointment. After I sat in the waiting room for hours, the nurse said, "If you think you're pregnant, the doctor doesn't need to see you for three or four months." I didn't think I was, but having only one ovary tended to make my monthly cycle unpredictable. I knew the doctor didn't want to see patients until they had missed several periods, so I left, feeling confused.

That night, while dining with friends, I began to

hemorrhage. James called the doctor and was told to get me home and in bed. "She may be pregnant and trying to miscarry." I rested for four days, and the bleeding stopped.

When I saw the doctor, he was visibly upset that the nurse had sent me home from the appointment without seeing him. A test confirmed my pregnancy, but we didn't know how far along I was. When I left his office, I was in shock. At the age of twenty-eight, unable to conceive for years, I was expecting a baby! I was excited but fearful when my doctor prescribed special injections every two weeks to prevent a possible miscarriage.

By the second trimester, the baby was growing fast, and I felt terrific. The doctor gave me a possible due date of November 22, which was my birthday, but said we couldn't know for sure.

I continued to feel good, so I inquired about having natural childbirth. My doctor was reserved in discussing it and said he could not recommend it. I wondered if he had concerns about my labor and delivery, so I dropped the subject. By mid-November, I was very large and had begun dilating.

On Friday, November 17, James left to go out of town in a small plane with Pop Hale, but bad weather forced them to turn back. As they tried to reschedule, James felt the time could coincide with my going into labor. He suggested I call and see if the doctor would check me. I knew my doctor wouldn't see me at 4:00 P.M. on a Friday afternoon, but I phoned the office when James persisted. I was surprised when the doctor agreed to check me and even more shocked when he said, "Let's induce you tomorrow morning. You are dilated enough."

November 18 was a long day of labor, but Robin was finally born around 5:30 P.M.. She weighed 7 pounds, 15 ounces, and had James' and Rhonda's dark hair and eyes. James told me later they couldn't get her to breathe for thirty minutes because her lungs were full of fluid. Her color was still blue when he saw her in the incubator. The doctor described her, at birth, as a "miracle baby." He said that, on a scale of one to ten, her chances of being normal would have been at a level two! And yet, after overcoming the problems during her birth, Robin was my healthiest child, with an abundance of energy and a temperament that charmed the entire family.

After Robin's birth, God gave us a peace that our family was complete. We could see God's wisdom in bringing each of our children in the time and order he had selected: two daughters by birth, and a specially chosen son through adoption.

As I watched my children grow, my faith in God's wisdom and love became stronger. I could understand my heavenly Father's heart toward me better, because I understood a parent's unconditional love.

CHAPTER NINE

ℱRIGHTENED AT THE TOP

WHEN ROBIN, OUR YOUNGEST CHILD, WAS FIVE OR SIX YEARS OLD, I took the old shoe box from my closet and looked through the tattered envelopes stuffed with love letters James had written to me during his first semester of college. I wanted to read them and capture again the image of his purity and passion toward the Lord. Many years had passed since he wrote them, but the pattern of his letters was still familiar—a brief description of his day, then a detailed account of his visit with the Lord from his special place in the piney woods. I especially loved his dialogue with Jesus.

I laid the box near me and chose a letter randomly, unfolded its yellowed pages, and read.

> *Betty, I went to the woods as soon as I could get away from class. I told Jesus how much I loved him and that I wanted to serve him. I thanked him for calling me to*

preach and for giving me boldness. God's presence saturated the place where I sat, and he seemed to say, "I've been waiting for you, James. I love you so much." I felt as if I could reach up and take him by the hand and walk with him. I told him, "I want to tell everyone how great you are."

74

In every letter James encouraged me to read a Scripture. This time it was a passage in Romans. *I'm sure I looked it up immediately*, I thought. Reading about what had inspired him seemed to bring me closer to him, although there were miles between us.

I read the next part a second time. *"Betty, please pray that I get an opportunity to preach soon."* Oh, how he longed to be preaching. That was all he thought about. And he witnessed everywhere he went. "God, I know you put that in him," I said as I prayed out loud.

The letter closed with James affectionately expressing his love for me. I recalled how I had memorized his encouraging words as an eighteen-year-old wearing his engagement ring. I missed him desperately. That letter was typical of all his letters. I reached for another. They were really love letters to God more than love letters to me. But something had happened over the past few years. His passion for Jesus had somehow dimmed. Where had that James Robison gone? With eager anticipation, I opened the next envelope.

Betty, God told me something today that totally stunned me. He told me he was going to use me to preach his

Word to the world. I told him I couldn't begin to think in those terms. I just wanted to tell people about him. Then he said, "Within a year, you will be preaching in the largest churches in America." I reminded God that I was just a teenager and I hadn't even preached in a church yet.

"You will preach in football stadiums and coliseums all over America," he said.

I told him, "I have only preached one time on a flatbed truck in Pasadena," but God said, "James, this will happen. I am going to use you."

I dropped to my knees and told God that he didn't have to give me a big ministry like that. Then he gave me a vision of what it was going to be like. I saw huge churches, stadiums, and coliseums. I stood before the crowds that filled them, preaching, and when I extended an invitation for people to come and receive Christ, thousands responded and surrounded the platform.

I was so overwhelmed I could hardly take it all in. I told him, "Jesus, all I care about is just you and me, right here. No matter what happens, if you give me a big ministry or a small one, I promise I'll always come right back here to you and tell you that I love you and I will wait upon you."

I paused and read that line again: *"I'll always come right back here to you and tell you that I love you."* Tears filled my eyes as I held the letter tightly in my hand. *Oh, God, nearly everything you showed him in the woods that day has happened. He has preached in football stadiums, large coliseums, and thousands have trusted Christ at every city-*

75

wide crusade. You have been faithful; you've kept your word. Why didn't James keep his promise to you? Why doesn't he seem to love intimate time alone with Jesus? Why does he seem easily irritated and even lustful?

I sobbed as I moved to my knees beside the bed. *Lord, why is he so defeated when you have blessed us so much? You've given us three wonderful children. We have a nice home, many gifted employees, and an airplane to transport our team and family. You've led James into a successful television ministry and friendships with great spiritual and national leaders, yet I have never seen him more miserable. He says he doesn't care if he ever preaches another sermon. What is happening to him? He asked me to pray that he would die in his sleep. I can't do what he asked. I could never pray for him to die. How can I help him? He has always been the confident leader I leaned on. Now he's leaning on me, and I am not strong enough.*

I cried with a hurt so deep I thought my heart might stop beating. I grabbed a tissue and leaned against the bed. I explored the past and tried to identify when everything had changed. What happened to make James feel separated from God? It couldn't have been a single event. It must have been a progression as he got busy fulfilling people's expectations. His passion to serve the Lord drove him to accept most of the requests for citywide crusades. He seldom turned down an invitation, and a pattern evolved. There was a week of preaching, a few days at home, followed by a full eight-day crusade, during which he would speak at least five or six times a day.

During the day he met with pastors and leaders, and

did radio and television appearances to promote the meeting. Then the urgent needs of teenagers pressed him to schedule several public school assemblies on the weekdays throughout the city.

Gradually over several months the atmosphere in our home had become more intense, and I was overwhelmed with the challenges from James' confessions. *At least he still communicates with me. I don't have to guess what he's experiencing or thinking.* He was his usual transparent self when he returned from every meeting. He wasted no time in giving me a vivid picture of his turmoil.

"It is like my mind is on fire," he would confess to me. "And I can't seem to control my thoughts or my appetite. I have become obsessed with playing hours of golf or tennis every day, and when I see a beautiful woman, I often have lustful thoughts. I go for days without reading my Bible, and I have totally abandoned my prayer time with the team. If I pray before I walk up to the pulpit, it is usually to beg God to let someone else preach."

I understood the growing obsession with sports. Although he was a gifted, competitive athlete, his mother had refused to allow him to participate in any school athletics when he was growing up . . . except for his last two years of high school after he moved in with Brother and Mrs. Hale.

He acts like he has something to prove to everyone and himself, I thought. *If he has an hour between ministry commitments, he fills it with golf, tennis, or basketball.*

The last time he played tennis, I had gone with him,

77

just so we could spend time together. But I regretted it. His temper was explosive. He threw his racket and raised his voice accusingly at his opponent, usually a staff person, when the game didn't go as he desired. But sports had also begun to enslave him when he was home for the few days between meetings.

If he is giving time to the Lord, reading his Bible or praying, I am not seeing it, I thought. *That's got to be the thing that robbed him of his joy. He stopped making time for fellowship with the Lord.* But I certainly didn't feel qualified to preach to him about maintaining the intimacy he had once had with God. I had never come close to experiencing what he described in his letters. I did all the right things, religiously. I read Scripture, prayed desperate prayers, but I never felt the powerful presence of God. I never heard God speak to me the way James had. *Why would anyone abandon that kind of fellowship with God if he was privileged enough to have it?*

James' struggle with lustful thoughts also really concerned and puzzled me. I couldn't understand that part of his torment, and it broke my heart. I didn't think badly of him, but I felt helpless. I would ask, "Am I doing something wrong?" James would always assure me that it wasn't my fault, but the accusing thoughts would come when he shared his frustrations. *Yeah, it's you. You are not capable of being the kind of wife he needs,* my subconscious mind would shout at me.

Meanwhile, I was having my own internal problems—the same old fear that nagged me into rejecting myself as James' partner in ministry. He needed me to be strong, but how could I help him when I was struggling? Because I knew he'd be worried about me, I chose not to tell him how I was feeling.

I rose from my knees, folded the letters, stuffed them in the box, and put them back in the closet. A glance at the clock told me I still had an hour before I needed to pick James up at the airport. *He's piloting the plane right now. Thank God he is not alone. Joe Simmons is with him.*

I knew that Joe usually tried to encourage James when he felt defeated. Besides praying for James, that was all I could do too—remind James how much his children and I needed and loved him. Most of all, I tried to convince him that God loved him and still had a purpose for his life.

As I waited for James beside the car at the small airport, it seemed dark and abandoned, except for one man tying down the twin-engine plane. James got in the passenger side of our car and insisted I drive. As I slipped in on the driver's side, he slumped down like he was totally exhausted.

"Are you sick?" I asked. He was frequently ill with throat infections and unexplainable aches and pains, but the doctors couldn't find anything wrong. And all the prescribed medications had proven unsuccessful in curing his chronic problems.

He didn't answer for a few minutes; then I heard a slow, choked response. "Tonight I pointed the plane toward the ground; I really wanted to kill myself. For a moment I didn't even care that Joe would have died with me, but he began screaming and pleading for me to pull back on the controls. I realized that it wasn't fair for me to make him and his family suffer because of my despair. So I pulled up on the controls. I am a living dead man, Betty. I have come to the end of myself physically, emotionally, mentally, and spiritually." He leaned forward and gripped his head in his hands.

I was so frightened that I didn't know how to respond. I couldn't believe he had succumbed to such defeat. Had he even thought of the children and me when he put the plane into a suicidal dive?

The next day he was on the phone for hours. I could tell some of the calls were long distance, because he kept the television volume low. The kids busied themselves in activities with friends. They seemed to sense he was more troubled than usual. I prayed that a breakthrough would somehow come—and soon.

James shared with me his desire to meet privately with a Florida pastor named Peter Lord. He said that Peter had described what he was experiencing, and said it was possible to be totally free.

I could see how desperately he wanted to believe what he was repeating to me. It was a small ray of hope from someone James had great confidence in. "I know I can trust him to keep things confidential," James reassured me.

Peter was a favorite speaker at our annual Bible conference. His preaching was unconventional but anointed. He was charming and gracious, with a fearless and nonreligious approach to ministry. The church he pastored developed a special prayer-and-counseling outreach for ministers and their families. They provided living quarters on the church property in beautiful Fort Lauderdale, Florida, to restore preachers who needed special encouragement and spiritual refreshing.

"You should do what Peter suggests," I coaxed. "Is your schedule clear where you could go soon?"

"I have to clear some time, and I need to do it right away," James stated firmly.

I knew he needed to go alone. The arrangements were made when a tiny hole opened in his schedule while conducting a crusade in Miami. He never left my thoughts the whole time he was away. I prayed fervently.

When he returned home, I could see a peace in his eyes. There was a hunger for the Word of God and a renewed zeal to preach what he had learned.

As usual, he was quick to give me a personal and detailed description of the ministry he received. Peter had shown James that Christians could be adversely affected by the powers of darkness—that evil spirits could torment and influence the actions of believers.

"James, I always thought if a Christian had Jesus in his heart, the devil and demonic spirits couldn't bother him," I said in surprise. "Is Peter saying Satan and his fallen angels can negatively attack a Christian?"

"That is exactly what Peter is saying. And he gave me some material to see it for myself in the Scriptures."

James listened to tapes and studied every spare moment during the weeks that followed. He definitely had experienced something. He had real hope for freedom. The change was obvious.

However, when he shared what he was learning with some well-known ministers, they laughed and belittled Peter Lord's teaching as absurd. James was disturbed by the attitudes and opinions expressed so adamantly, but peer pressure prevailed. He quit pursuing the breakthrough he desired in his spiritual life.

Within a short time the peace in his eyes was gone, and his torment returned with a vengeance. It was as if the enemy that had been driven out had returned and brought seven more demons with him.

CHAPTER TEN

FREEDOM'S PATH

NORMALLY THE BIBLE CONFERENCE WAS THE HIGHLIGHT OF OUR year—for us as well as our faithful supporters. The staff planned a conference in Houston, Texas, celebrating twenty years in ministry. But this time, neither James nor I was mentally or spiritually prepared for such a special event.

After two days of meetings I was weary, but we still had another full day to go. Our children attended the sessions with us, and I could see they were tired as well. I decided we needed a break, so the kids and I stayed in the hotel room on Saturday morning. During lunch James came to check on us.

"You really missed it," he said with more passion than I'd heard in his voice for a while. "God spoke through Dudley Hall this morning. He brought the most powerful message I've ever heard. He is speaking again this afternoon. You should go."

Dudley had been a close friend for many years. We

often socialized with him and his wife, Betsy. James had a lot of confidence in Dudley's knowledge of the Bible, so he frequently talked with him about ministry. He had also felt free to discuss his personal struggles with Dudley.

It didn't take much coaxing to get me there for Dudley's next message. His humorous yet practical teaching style, combined with his country-boy charm, made him one of my personal favorites.

The worship service had already started when we arrived, so the kids and I sat near the back. As soon as the music ended, Dudley walked to the pulpit. It was his custom to open with a comical story, then smoothly transition to exhorting us with three dynamic points and a stirring closing. This time he began with a personal testimony and shared how God was changing him with the power of his Word.

Dudley had been in an extended crusade in Dothan, Alabama, and rumors were circulating that the people who attended wouldn't let the meetings end. But because several preachers took turns ministering, Dudley had been free to fly to Texas for our conference. As he spoke he described the ministry in Alabama as a divine encounter with the power of God. "I don't know how long it will continue—I guess until God is through," he explained. "The news has spread, and people are coming from many miles away to get in on what God is doing."

I watched the people seated near me. No one displayed the usual afternoon drowsiness or restlessness. The audience was focused—eager to hear the exciting news about God's powerful presence.

"Every time we meet, there is an atmosphere charged with a heightened illumination of truth," Dudley continued. "Jim Hylton, a pastor from Fort Worth, Texas, has preached a number of times on the most obscure passages of Scripture, and people are getting deep revelation from each message. There are unexpected miracles happening. People tell us afterward, 'I noticed that my pain left me during the praise service last night, and it hasn't returned. God healed me.' Some young men who attended told us they were delivered from their drug addictions during the preaching. The leaders haven't created a special prayer service for such things. God is simply doing the work in our midst, and we learn about it afterward."

I tried to picture what he described, but I had never experienced anything like it in all our years of ministry. Nor could I relate to Dudley's passion to return and attend a meeting for weeks on end. *How can families manage attending services night after night? How does Betsy endure such a long separation from her husband?*

Dudley's message referenced many Scriptures to support his points. I marked the ones describing miracles and supernatural acts. I sat on the edge of my seat, not wanting to miss a word. Steadily his voice intensified with a commanding authority. *James was right,* I thought. *Dudley is different.*

As he continued I heard words like *strongholds, avoiding deception,* and *casting down imaginations.* He talked about the effect Satan can have on a Christian's life. There was so much I didn't understand. I was confused by the many Old Testament references and wondered how his message would affect James. Certain aspects of his sermon reminded me of the teaching by Peter Lord and his staff. And yet Peter's words had stirred such controversy between James and fellow ministers that it was difficult to hear and follow the Lord. *Is Dudley opening himself to the same rebuke and criticism?* I wondered. *Since he's teaching this at our conference, will James go through the harassment all over again?*

"I have to confess," Dudley said in closing, "in the past I have let pleasing man influence my decision to minister the truth of God's Word. I compromised to avoid controversy. Satan's lies have tormented my mind and assaulted God's truth, but that is over, folks. I am totally free." I looked to the left side of the platform where James sat. He slumped heavily, his elbows resting on his knees and his face buried in his hands. I hurt for him.

Dudley asked all of us to bow our heads for prayer. There was a solemn stillness throughout the crowd—as if people were holding their breath. Now what would happen? I sheepishly glanced around and wondered if everyone felt as apprehensive as I did. *Will miracles happen in this service?* I was puzzled, but I believed God had changed Dudley's life. *Perhaps this is what James needs. If our friend really has the answer, then I should press through my fear and encourage James to pursue whatever Dudley recommends.*

Weeks later, at a dinner with close friends Pete and Jody Claytor, Pete described in detail a man named Milton Greene, a simple carpet cleaner who taught the Bible with exceptional revelation to preachers and church leaders. They confirmed what Dudley had described at the Houston conference. Both ministers and laymen were experiencing the supernatural power of God.

"James," Pete said, "you ought to spend some time with Milt. He knows a lot about spiritual darkness and the effects the demonic world can have on Christians." I watched James become more uncomfortable as Pete pressed him to go. James was curious, but he stopped short of making a firm commitment. "I might go see him, but I really don't know when I'd have time."

I knew what would hold me back—the fear of the unknown. The whole spiritual darkness discussion made my skin crawl. I'd always believed if I left the devil alone, he wouldn't bother me. Their talk about Milton Greene's ministry gave me chills, and a voice inside warned, *Don't go near this man.*

A week later I had fallen asleep on the couch while James talked at length on the phone. It was becoming a daily pattern in his frustrating search for answers. I was awakened suddenly by James' loud voice. "I don't believe it! Dudley just hung up on me. He was mad. He told me to quit calling him if I wasn't going to make an effort to get with Milton Greene to get some help. He said the man could show me things in the Word and pray with me. The guy is just a layman who cleans carpets, but Dudley says he knows about these things I'm experiencing. What do you think I should do?"

I should have said, "Stay away." That's the way I had been thinking. Yet from my heart came surprising words:

"Several trustworthy friends have told us Milton Greene can help you. We both have prayed and begged God to send you some counsel. There's nothing I can do. That's for sure. I think you should go see him."

James set the time and the place, but I could see he struggled with his decision. Milton was to travel with the team for a series of meetings. James' disagreeable mood seemed to intensify until the day he left. I was anxious about the whole ordeal, but we had put things in motion. There was no turning back.

Each day when James called, I asked, "Have you spent any time with Milt?" And he would answer, "No, we've both been too busy. Maybe tomorrow." Finally, near the end of their trip, Milt asked to pray with him and show him some things in the Word. The next day James told me what happened.

"Milt said I am the most tormented man he has ever met." James chuckled.

"What did he do?"

"He read some Scriptures, then asked if he could pray for me. He took the desk chair and placed it in the middle of the room, then gestured for me to sit down. It looked like the electric chair to me, but I sat in it, wondering what was about to happen. He stood behind me, quoting long passages of Scripture as he prayed. At one point his voice switched gears and got louder. I worried about the team hearing his prayer through the walls as he rebuked Satan and every tormenting spirit."

"So what happened?" I asked anxiously.

"Nothing. And I really wanted something to happen.

I told him I didn't feel a thing. That didn't faze him. He just smiled and said, 'Son, it's all over; the traffic is gonna stop.' And I had no idea what he meant."

The next night James flew home and came to bed late. I was surprised when he woke me in the early hours of the morning, weeping with joy. "Betty, something has happened—in my heart and my mind. That claw in my brain is gone. I can think—my mind is clear."

If I had any doubts about the reality of what happened, the doubts were soon removed. The tormenting thoughts really *were* gone. James had radically changed! I didn't know my own husband. He had constant joy. The children were amazed at the peaceful atmosphere he created in our home. He pored over Scripture and made it a priority to minister to others who suffered as he had.

I was happy about what was happening to him, but I was also fearful. Would this last? We had tried other things before, and nothing had worked. So the change in him actually frightened me. I even tested him by trying to pick fights in the weeks that followed. But he would say, "That's okay, honey." His sweetness and patient love left the burden on me. I realized *I'm the only one in this argument.*

I started having severe headaches and experiencing deep fatigue. Every day I would finish my housework and then collapse on the sofa, drained of energy and crying from the pain in my head. It seemed I had nothing left to give toward relationships, and that included my time with God.

One day Robin, who was now ten or eleven years old, interrupted my vigil on the couch. "Mom, I made this for you." She handed me a card drawn on construction paper, with pretty flowers on the front. Opening it, I read, *"Dear Mom, I am praying that you will get well soon. PS: Maybe God is trying to tell you something."*

I thanked her and, as soon as she left the room, quickly closed the card. My head was pounding as the words of her postscript tormented me. I asked James, "Do you think God is trying to show me something?"

He hesitated, then answered, "Yeah." Then he moved over to the sofa.

Somehow I managed to sit up next to him. I pleaded, "Please, tell me what God is showing you."

"Well, I don't think you are going to like it," he said.

"I don't care. You can tell me anything, and I will accept it."

"Okay," he said slowly. "I think God is saying that you have an unteachable spirit."

Suddenly I felt a boost of energy. I stood up, put my hands on my hips, and announced, "I do not!" I ran to the bedroom, hurt and upset. Moments later I heard James say he was taking the kids to play tennis.

I paced angrily around my room, glaring at the walls. The room grew cold with an eerie presence. I was wide awake but saw evil, impish faces on the walls and in the dresser mirror. Their mouths curled up in taunting smirks, and their voices mocked me in my thoughts: *You can't get out of this. I have you now. You can't escape.* I was so frightened I wanted to scream or run, but I did neither. My limbs felt paralyzed as the images ambushed me on every turn, and their heckling grew louder. The pain between my eyes increased till I thought my head would explode. *This must be what demons are like,* I thought, terrified.

I fell to my knees beside the bed. "Please, God, help me. Make these things go away. I'll do whatever you say." I wept and confessed, "I *do* have an unteachable spirit. Please forgive me."

When I opened my eyes, the images had disappeared. I walked to the mirror, and all I saw was my reflection. A relaxed smile came to my face when I realized my headache was gone.

I shared my experience with James, and he encouraged me to study a booklet called *Blockages to Communication.*[1] It contained Scriptures and thoughts compiled to help people understand how the enemy works, and the confessions of who we are in Christ. I looked up the verses outlined in each section, and the mental block I'd always felt when I read God's Word disappeared. Soon I was reading beyond the suggested verses and covering entire chapters at each sitting. God was planting his Word in my heart.

Sometime later Milton Greene and his wife, Joyce, were in the Fort Worth area, near Jim Hylton's church. One evening they came to our home for dinner and fellowship. I listened as Milt and James sat with open

---

[1]For a copy of *Blockages to Communication: Keys to Repentance,* compiled by James Robison (Fort Worth, TX: LIFE Outreach International, 1982, 1995), write: LIFE Outreach International, P.O. Box 982000, Forth Worth, TX 76182-8000. This material also includes some material by Kay Arthur, now adapted and included in the book entitled *How Can I Live: A Devotional Journey with Kay Arthur* by Kay Arthur (New Jersey: Fleming H. Revell).

Bibles in their laps, discussing the Scriptures. I don't remember what they were talking about, but fear began to grip me. I felt threatened and anxious. Milt kept looking my way, smiling as he listened to James talk. Finally, he asked, "Excuse me, Betty. Could you and I go to the kitchen table for a little talk?" My heart moved to my throat, but I nodded. In a conversational manner, he opened his Bible and asked me to read verses that he pointed to, all related to fear. As I read I began to shake violently, and Milt responded by praying and quoting Scripture. He calmly explained that a spirit of fear was controlling much of my life. I held on to the table, and it shook with me. *Why can't I stop this trembling?* I wondered. Finally Milt quit praying, and my hands became steady.

"Betty, you just keep studying God's Word and praying. God will bring this to pass. Now don't you worry about it. You rest in him."

I had taken a big step. The fear and insecurity I had always lived with was now exposed. Anyone who knew me well had seen the hold it had on me. Until that night I thought the fearful thoughts were entirely my own, but they weren't. I realized that for most of my life, I had been the target of the devil's lies. Now I knew how to recognize them.

In the days that followed I did what Milton suggested. I read the Word faithfully and exercised faith in the truth I learned.

Late one night James and I fell into bed, exhausted from a long day of ministry but spiritually refreshed.

Tears suddenly flowed freely, overwhelming my emotions.

Tenderly James reached for me. "What's wrong, honey?"

I turned and faced him. "God is just loving me. For the first time I feel like God is saying, 'Betty, I love you like you are. I'm pleased with you. You let me do the changing in you. Quit trying to change yourself.' " I lay there for a long time, just letting God's love flow through me. I knew I didn't have to work for it anymore. God's Son had died to show me his love.

A few days later I was dressing for a service when the trembling started again. It was so severe that James had to help me get dressed. We prayed, and I boldly quoted Scripture from memory. I declared to the enemy that freedom from the stronghold of fear was mine because of the victory of Jesus. Gradually the shaking diminished until I felt it leave. The deliverance was complete.

That evening in the service, I was like a bird let out of a cage. I worshiped the Lord with a freedom I had never known. It was truly a washing of my spirit. I actually felt God holding me in his arms. For the first time in my life I was convinced—God's powerful love would never leave me.

CHAPTER ELEVEN

NOT HERE . . . NOT NOW

FINALLY FEELING THE POWER OF GOD'S LOVE AND A DELIVERANCE from fear didn't mean, however, that my life became automatically perfect. As a shy person at heart and in temperament, I still struggled with having to be in the limelight. But more and more, James wanted me to share his ministry. He wanted me to travel with him, to be on the stage with him. I would have preferred to be in the background.

If I had to be onstage, I preferred to make my entrance with James and the others. The front row of the guest seating was where I sat from the time the music started until the last speaker finished. I knew the camera focused more often on me if James was preaching and any reference to our personal lives prompted the director's cues to catch my reaction. I tried to pay close attention to James so my smiles were timely and I wasn't caught unaware. But being in the limelight was exhausting to me.

Our annual Bible conference offered three days of morning, afternoon, and evening sessions. The meetings had gained a reputation over the years for being inspiring but long. By the second day, I was usually weary. But I endured, not because I was Mrs. James Robison, but because I didn't want to miss a word. It was obvious; the people seated throughout the arena felt the same way. Each speaker challenged us. James sat forward in his seat, or stood and shouted, "Yes, that's right!" in support of the man at the podium. My heart had been stirred too, but I guarded any visible display of emotion. Showing emotion onstage was, to me, like revealing myself and my secrets before the world. James was comfortable with it; I was not.

One day while onstage with James, I stole a glance at the TV monitor on the floor just beyond my feet. It was clear my hair needed a touch-up and my makeup needed freshening. Hoping to be less noticeable, I sat very still in my chair—one of eight in the designated seating on the large stage. The speakers for our conference occupied the other chairs. Usually the cameraman closed in on the faces of the other speakers—Jack Hayford, Dudley Hall, or Rick Godwin—as they listened to James' message. However, this time I was startled to see the camera focused on *me* instead.

My heart began to pound. I turned my body and posed myself where I could watch James as he spoke and still shift my eyes down to the monitor for another quick peek.

Oh, great. Look at my eyes! A tight shot of my face

revealed extremely fatigued eyes that were now staring down, unfocused. The audiovisual director must have seen my frown as I studied my image, so he quickly changed back to James. But the picture of my tired eyes remained frozen in my mind.

There was nothing I could do. The dinner break had been so hurried. Our makeup artist had begged for time to remove the early morning application. "You've been under those television lights all day," she advised. "We need to start over." But the clock told us there was only time to add a third layer of powder and fresh lipstick if I wanted to walk onstage with James.

Now camera two zoomed in to project my image on the large screen before the arena's eight thousand pairs of eyes. Sloppy posture, fidgeting in my chair, heavy eyelids—everything about me could be observed under the television lights. There was never a moment to relax or stretch when the red lights on top of the camera were lit.

The service is almost over. Sit up and smile. Focus on the people who are coming for prayer, I told myself.

As James finished his sermon, he invited those who needed prayer or counseling to come forward. There was no music to play on the crowd's feelings as the message closed. "Let's hold the music until after they have come forward for prayer," James said. The musicians agreed with him. No one wanted to manipulate or stir up emotional decisions.

I watched most of the crowd stand and slip past the small number who remained seated. With no instruments and no singing, all I heard was the sound of seats folding up and feet moving on the hard concrete floor. In a solemn, thunderous surrender they came from the aisles of the upper sections, and the numbers multiplied to thousands as they moved down to cover the arena floor and press against the platform.

As people crowded forward, I studied their faces and gave an approving smile to a woman near the steps. Her eyes were fixed on me. I sensed that her composure masked a tormented prisoner. Feeling her pain, I closed my eyes and prayed for her. And then there were others I was guided to pray for. But I never left my chair to do it.

That's what I do best, I thought. *I pray. I don't need to speak in front of all these people.* Then a worry struck: *I hope James won't call on me to say a word at the close tonight.* The thought of speaking to the crowd stirred deep anxiety in me, so I directed my attention back to the service. I noticed every camera had turned and focused on James behind the podium or those standing near him on the floor. Now I could relax and watch the people.

Oh, Lord, show them how much you love them . . . the way you did me, I prayed.

The soft acoustic instruments began to play, and our singer hummed the melody of a familiar worship song. I wanted to harmonize on the alto part, as I did in congregational worship. No one joined her, so I kept silent. The lyrics played in my head: *"Living water, fill my thirsty soul."* My heart began to swell with emotion, with love for my Lord. Had no one been watching, I could have assumed my practice as a child in our side yard, dancing freely while singing songs to the Lord.

With my eyes closed and my hands open before me, I felt the warmth of God's presence. In my mind I revisited my most intimate and private worship, when alone in my living room. The times when I heard God say, *"Betty, worship me now."*

Then suddenly I knew I was hearing the Lord's voice on this stage. But I resisted. *Not here . . . not now.* In an arena filled with people, I couldn't express my praise like I did at home. *Please God . . . don't ask me to do that,* I begged. *I would embarrass James and myself. What would everyone think?*

I was relieved when James began speaking again and the music faded to a faint underscoring. He asked Jack, Dudley, and Rick to come and pray for him. As the ministers moved in close, James explained to the crowd, "I need your prayers because God has given me a strong message for the church. Some people aren't going to be happy about it. I'll have to stand strong and speak the truth, regardless of the criticism."

Touched by his humility, the people in the audience remained still as the three ministers bowed their heads to pray.

That's when I recalled my conversation with James weeks before. We discussed the many changes our ministry had experienced since last year's conference. Now in our mid-forties, James and I believed we were facing more difficulties and major changes. We also felt that soon we would experience a departure from everything comfortable and familiar.

"Lord, give James courage and boldness," the youngest speaker prayed aloud. Suddenly his words stirred fear of what God would require of me. I comforted myself with a hopeful prayer: *Surely I can trust you, Lord, to protect me from embarrassment as I walk through these changes in support of my husband.*

The excitement built throughout the arena as each minister voiced his request and praised God for the way he would use James in our nation. James leaned over the podium with his head buried in his hands. The atmosphere of the room was charged with faith when God spoke to me again: *"Abandon yourself to worship me."*

My hands trembled as I bowed my head and covered my face. I whispered my willingness to obey but hoped God would not require it of me.

When the prayers ended, James leaned weakly on the pulpit, unable to speak. The men didn't leave the stage but repositioned themselves to the back of the platform, where they stood gazing over the arena. Everyone waited in silence. God's love pressed so near that I held my breath as our soloist, Jeanne Rogers, sang. I could feel the echo of the song's words in my heart: *"Bread of Life . . . feed my aching need. Holy Spirit, come."*

The heat from the television lights overhead intensified, seeming to illuminate the large center section of the stage. Then I felt a hand touch my shoulder, and a chill ran down my back. I stood—no, *leaped*—to obey. Suddenly the crowd seemed a million miles off. The stage became an isolated world—just like the side yard of my childhood—where nothing mattered except my expression of love to the Lord.

My movements resembled one approaching a majestic throne. With hands outstretched before me, I stepped into the presence of royalty. I bowed and whirled, encircling the large open stage with the innocent abandon I had known as a little girl. I danced, as much at ease as if worshiping in the privacy of our living room. The patterns and steps were not choreographed by my mind but spontaneous movement I felt inspired to do. There were times I danced with my eyes closed, yet knew later I had crossed near speakers and musicians without stumbling.

101

My hand movements interpreted the words that I mouthed, while the singing continued:

For I am nothing without your love;
    breathe new life in me.
Then will my life bring glory unto Thee.
Holy Spirit . . . Oh Holy Spirit . . .
    Sweet Holy Spirit, come.

Then the song ended. As abruptly as I had leaped at the touch on my shoulder, I fell to my knees, void of strength and filled with embarrassment. What had I done? My body trembled, and I buried my face in the carpet as I wept. How could I have been so foolish to interrupt the service?

I felt an arm across my shoulders. "Oh, Betty." Jeanne knelt beside me in a supportive embrace. "That was beautiful."

Still I could not look up.

She spoke in a comforting tone. "Don't you know you have pleased the Lord and blessed everyone who saw you?"

As I tried to dry my eyes, I explained, "The moment that person behind me touched my shoulder, I knew I had to obey God."

"Betty," Jeanne answered, "no one was behind you. I was watching you the whole time I sang. You simply stepped out and began dancing gracefully."

"Then who touched me on the shoulder?" I asked, puzzled. Then I realized, with awe, that I had felt the touch of God Almighty himself, calling me to worship him freely.

To the amazement of all, many people in the audience began coming forward, falling on their knees in worship and repentance as they experienced the awesome presence of God.

*T*HE WALLFLOWER RELEASED

I STOOD IN LINE WITH THE OTHER WOULD-BE BALLERINAS, dressed in a black leotard and tights. We were directed to place our hand on the wooden bar, as our graceful, young teacher demonstrated movements and called out lovely French words. I glanced at the mirror covering the wall beside us. We were a small class of beginners—all adult women near my age.

My confidence grew with each lesson. As I focused on my image in the mirror, I no longer felt like such a novice. I straightened my back and pointed my toes. *I don't look too bad doing ballet. I wonder if the others are fulfilling a lifelong dream too.* I had no desire to perform, but I enjoyed using what I was learning when I worshiped the Lord in my living room.

At last, fear and insecurity no longer controlled me. I was free to express myself—free to be me. I took great pleasure in pursuing things I'd lacked the courage to attempt before. Worshiping God with my whole being was my first bold expression of freedom. Since I needed to express my gratitude and celebrate the joy I had discovered, I played worship music a lot at home. I sang loudly, lifting my hands as I danced—leaping, twirling, and bowing. I was no longer embarrassed to express my heart to the Lord even when James and the kids were home.

104

Often my daughter Robin joined me when I put the praise music on. Moving freely with grace and energy, she had exhibited a passion for dance the moment she learned that Scripture recorded it as worship. After her first lesson, her dance teacher said she was a natural.

At the age of thirteen Robin was featured in a worship ballet at our Bible conference. James and I wept and praised God even in the preview Robin gave us in our living room. Our other daughter, Rhonda, sang with the accompaniment of live orchestra as her younger sister danced on the large stage. The presentation was dramatic and inspiring. We were happy to see our daughters use their talents so boldly.

James began to share freely with our Bible conference audience how God had worked in my life and set me free from fear and insecurity. As a result, I received an invitation to share my testimony with a ladies group in West Texas. In the past I would have automatically rejected the idea of speaking publicly, but with James' encouragement, I overcame my timidity enough to share my testimony. The response was so positive that I decided to give prayerful consideration to future invitations.

My family was still my first priority, but it was apparent God was adding ministry opportunities to my schedule. James and I often spent time with preachers and their wives who felt there was no one they could trust with their problems. I learned there were many women who also lived, as I had for so many years, imprisoned by people's expectations and a paralyzing fear of failure. I gained confidence in offering counsel and personally praying for them.

The freedom James and I experienced affected the circles of people around us. Our desire to study the Word of God and walk in the power and fullness of the Holy Spirit spread to our staff and thrilled many friends. However, among the more traditional, evangelical supporters a controversy erupted that launched an organized and well-publicized attack against our ministry. Outspoken leaders of our denomination chose to boycott some of our meetings and encouraged their congregations to do likewise.

Although James and I both felt rejection and hurt from the loss of close friendships, the experience also gave James a passionate message that called for the unity of believers. He preached against judging and challenged Christians to get beyond any petty, doctrinal differences. He begged them not to rip and divide, but come together in a bond of peace, love, and unity in Christ. He lived what he preached by reaching out to the men who privately and/or openly criticized him in news articles and denominational gatherings. He offered them forgiveness and friendship.

105

Yet still our ministry declined; we lost over 50 percent in support. We were forced to make cutbacks in staff and television production, but we never hesitated to talk about the freedom we enjoyed. We filled our calendar with seminars of intensive, scriptural studies to help Christians know the power and authority over Satan they had through Christ.

People of all denominations were taught how to have an intimate relationship with Jesus and to be proactive and alert in their faith. In large meetings across the country, James preached the same clear word of salvation through Jesus, but he broadened the message to show people how God heals, delivers, and wants to fill them with the power of the Holy Spirit.

God rewarded our commitment to love, forgive, and never compromise the truth. Every plan of our opposition became an opportunity for greater outreach. The support we had lost was replaced within one year. The media attention, initiated to promote negative press, had an opposite effect, increasing the popularity of our program, and broadening the age and demographics of our viewing audience. Every conference and seminar grew in attendance, and many more lives were being changed.

My time alone with God took on new dimensions as I rose early in the morning to pray and study. I was excited to learn I could hear God and understand his Word for myself. At times I felt confident enough to share my insights with James and then was shocked to see him use them as sermon themes.

The Old Testament no longer intimidated me. It was like a treasure hunt each time I opened to the left side of my Bible. My new challenge was stopping my search once I started. References in the books of the prophets and the historical account of the children of Israel connected me to the fulfillment of God's promises in the New Testament. I was obsessed with seeing truth and hearing for myself what God's purposes were in the stories I had known since childhood.

Studying the Word brought many changes to my thinking. My faith in God grew, and I learned how to obtain and enjoy his rest. I stopped trying to create peace and trusted Christ for it. Scripture made it clear that God had already provided everything I needed for life and godliness. Hebrews 11:6 convinced me that *without faith it is impossible to please Him, for he who comes to God must believe that He is, and that He is a rewarder of those who diligently seek Him.*

I armed myself with effective battle plans to resist the whisperings of my adversaries. I understood and accepted Christ as the perfect revelation of God, the final and complete sacrifice for sin. I didn't have to earn God's love or favor, because my heavenly Father accepted me. What a freeing truth that was in my life!

God created us to be in relationship with him. He did everything he could to lovingly nurture the children of Israel. But I didn't read about many who sought to know him the way he wanted to be known. In John 17, I sensed the intimate bond between Jesus and his heavenly Father as he prayed for himself, his disciples, and future believers. He expressed his desire for them to be unified, protected from the evil one, and made pure and holy by words of truth:

> *I . . . pray . . . that they all may be one, as You, Father, are in Me, and I in You; that they also may be one in Us, that the world may believe that You sent Me. And the glory which You gave Me I have given them, that they may be one just as We are one: I in them, and You in Me; that they may be made perfect in one, and that the world may know that You have sent Me, and have loved them as You have loved me.*

My heart interpreted his request: *Jesus wants me to know the Father's love as he knew it. And, if he petitioned his Father for it, then it must be possible.* My heart ached to know the heavenly Father better, and I waited in stillness to hear him speak to me after I read my Bible and prayed. His voice penetrated my thoughts, and what he spoke was consistent with the truth I read in his Word. The closeness I gained reshaped my life and exposed more areas in need of deliverance. God revealed how pride had controlled me in the past and still worked to restrict me from complete obedience. Throughout my life I had avoided situations that might make me look foolish or where I might feel rejected. It was obvious that pride was the root of my fear and insecurity, and God was ready to tear down that stronghold as well.

I submitted my life to God's pruning and prayed, *Take me, and use me. Fill me with your Spirit and do what-*

ever you want with my life. I guess the Lord said, *"Okay, here we go,"* because the events that followed clearly set his ax to the root of that pride.

We were in the second day of a regional conference with two hundred of our most faithful partners. James and I sat with our children on the front row of a hotel conference room. During worship, the presence of the Holy Spirit rested heavily on me. And as Dudley Hall preached, I felt a growing anticipation of God's super-natural power enveloping me. It steadily increased until it became an electrical surge through my body. I kept thinking it would let up if I remained still and focused on the message, but it increased.

Soon the visible effects were obvious to James and others around me. I worried that my children would fear I was having a seizure or a heart attack. With all the strength I could muster I leaned over to James and whispered, "No matter what happens in the next few moments, tell the children not to be afraid. I am okay— God is doing something." When James got the word to them, they sat calmly—but their undivided attention was still on their mother.

Dudley was closing when I felt a gravitational force press against my body, pinning me to my chair. My face distorted with the impact of it, and I wept as the Holy Spirit's power overwhelmed me in intercession. My prayer for the condition of the church of Jesus Christ was represented in a vision of a crippled and twisted old woman. Though I couldn't move, I could hear weeping and praying throughout the room. A caring friend knelt on the floor and reached for me. I pulled back and warned, "Don't touch me!" My heavy eyelids closed, my lips were taut, and my body felt rigid. God spoke the warning through me to protect her from the energy flowing through me and to protect the vision from being interrupted.

Then Betsy Hall came to the microphone with a Scripture from the second chapter of Revelation. It recalled how God gave Jezebel a chance to repent of her sin, but she wouldn't. As a result, judgment came upon her. Betsy believed God was calling for repentance in the church in the same way, warning that there would be a window of time for the church to turn from its sin.

Her message confirmed what God was doing in our midst and set the stage for me to share the vision. The force of the electricity had been so engaging—like the swell of an enormous wave lifting and carrying my body while the Holy Spirit revealed the message I was to give. But as the powerful current gradually diminished, my body felt like it had been washed ashore, leaving me in a weakened condition. I whispered to James, "I have to speak." He practically carried me to the microphone and stood near, fearing I would collapse. I draped my upper body across the podium, stretched my arms around it, and held on. It took great effort to hold my head up and speak.

"Don't be afraid. What has happened to me is from the Lord." I paused as emotion choked my words. "God showed me a vision of a frail, shriveled-up old woman, lying helpless on a table. Her body was twisted and crippled, and her face was distorted. He told me, 'This is my church.' " Suddenly my knees buckled. James secured my body's twisted movements and helped me lean closer to the microphone. "God is crushed—brokenhearted over the condition of his children. He wants to revive them and strengthen them so they can move in his power toward his purpose for their lives. That can happen if we will shed all the things that distract us and pull us down. If we do, we will be able to demonstrate his love through us to others."

When I finished speaking, the people convulsed in deep wailing and brokenness. I had heard the term *travailing in the Spirit,* but had never seen it before. Some lay facedown, sobbing and pounding their fists. Others knelt, confessing the immorality of the church, and the hatred and jealousy among denominations. It continued for nearly fifteen minutes and then gradually softened to whispered prayers.

After a while there was a peaceful, holy atmosphere in the room, and people returned to their seats. No one spoke. They just waited in silence with their heads bowed.

Eventually James addressed the group, expressing his bewilderment. "I know my wife. She would be the last one in the world to want to draw attention to herself or disrupt a meeting. What has happened tonight was God. I have to confess, for a moment I was afraid she was dying, but she let me know that the Holy Spirit was doing something through her. Honestly, I have never seen anything like this. Tonight we have heard God's heart and how it breaks for the division he sees in his body. He showed us how pitiful and powerless his church is right now, and how ridiculous we look to the rest of the world. But I am encouraged because I sense he accomplished what he planned to do, and your prayers have set us on a new course. I think we are going to see some awesome changes in his church at large. Do you believe it too?"

Suddenly the room came alive with men and women voicing the hope they had in God to change the hearts of leaders in the church. Declarations of faith were made, exalting the authority of God and denouncing Satan's power to hold his church in deception. A celebration of God's triumph through Christ erupted, and loud singing and clapping were heard all over the room. I was excited, but no one would have known it by looking at me. I was sitting in my chair physically drained from the whole ordeal, but inside I rejoiced with all those around me.

Undeniable, life-changing miracles occurred in many couples' lives that night. The ministry suddenly surged forward with supernatural provision and direction. One young couple was so deeply moved by God's Spirit to support what God was doing that they wrote a check to the ministry for one million dollars.

"What a strange experience," a friend remarked the next morning. "I'm glad you were obedient and didn't resist what God was doing through you, Betty. We would have all missed a great blessing."

I smiled at her words and thought, *Lord, you brought me to the place where I could allow you to use me that way.*

My pride and my fear would have fought you tooth and nail had this happened a year ago. I yielded because I knew my Father and felt I could trust his love.

After that conference I caught James studying me like I was some mysterious person he hadn't known before. He had always expressed his love and admiration, but from that point, he spoke about it more frequently, praising me as a godly woman. Our spiritual communication became lengthy, stimulating discussions of Scripture—a level of exchange I thought only theologians shared with James.

113

Then one day he said, "Betty, I've been thinking. I would like for you to start traveling with me as much as possible. Rhonda is happily married. Randy and Robin are old enough to stay home by themselves. And I wish you would consider hosting the television show with me. How do you feel about that?"

I didn't dare respond with the negative thoughts that popped into my head. His request honored me so sweetly. He didn't press me for an answer. He knew our home was my comfort zone, and I would need some time to pray and work through the excuses.

Several days later God gave me clear direction that I was to be by James' side for as many personal appearances as possible. I wanted to be with him but struggled with leaving the kids so often. They were active teenagers who couldn't travel much because of their school and church involvement. Randy, an honor student, was active in sports, music, and drama. He was also president of the student body. Through Robin's nine years of public and private school she'd worked admirably in her studies, maintained respected leadership roles in various student organizations, and was enjoying being a cheerleader for all the athletic events. We supported their involvement as much as our schedule would allow, and I tried to attend events when James was out of town. To go with James meant depriving them of parental support for their activities. Before long Randy would graduate, and that would leave Robin at home alone.

The answer to these obstacles seemed obvious. We should let our intensely academic son finish his senior year and homeschool Robin on the road with us. We were shocked when Robin eagerly embraced the idea. It was obvious that Randy felt good about the confidence we placed in him to handle things while we were gone.

The family's decision forced me to deal with an insecurity that had haunted me since childhood. *You are dumb. You never excelled academically. Robin is only a teenager, and she is already more intelligent than you are. What can you teach your daughter? This is too much responsibility—you'd better back out now, before Robin gets her hopes too high.*

Though the thoughts swarmed like bees around my head, I dismissed them as lies. Many victories had been won since the night fear was defeated. I discovered I had the authority to cut off the tape the enemy played in my head and stand firmly upon the truth. *No! I am not dumb. I may not have done well in school, but things are different now. If Jesus is calling me to teach my daughter, then he will bless every effort I make to learn, and he will equip me to do it.*

I took the big step and ordered the curriculums. I gained confidence to instruct her and monitor her progress with the help of the Lord. Robin's confidence, interest in learning, and self-motivation made it an enjoyable task, whether we were traveling together with James or studying at home. As we tackled a variety of subjects, I developed interests that would have intimidated me before. One day I was so passionate about the history lesson that Robin interrupted my teaching fervor, pleading, "Mom, cool it, please!"

I know she was proud of her achievements when she finished high school more than a semester ahead of her friends. However, I'm convinced I gained more from our study experience than she did. I graduated in the assessment of my ability to learn.

Robin loved to be productive when she traveled with us. After she graduated, she busied herself assisting in any area of service to our staff. Unlike her mother, she looked forward to James introducing her to the audience. She always let him know afterward if he forgot. We were inspired by her boldness, and her faith and love for life. Our youngest child's closeness during those few years was a gift to James and me. We had never dreamed she would fall in love with the son of our dear friends, the Turners. At the age of nineteen she was ready to get married and move to Tulsa, Oklahoma.

The night before the wedding I reflected on all God had done in our family. Rhonda had married Terry Redmon, a godly young man she met at Baylor University. He brought creative leadership to several areas within the organization of our ministry. They blessed us with two precious grandchildren, Lora and Luke.

Randy had surprised us one weekend before starting his last year at Oral Roberts University. He brought home the lovely red-haired young lady that God had shown him would be his wife. He announced, "Mom, Debbie is like you!" We welcomed her to our family. They had married the week after they graduated and made their home in Tulsa, Oklahoma.

And now, Kenny Turner was the perfect husband for Robin, our youngest child. Older than Robin, Kenny had a promising future in his father's business. He surrounded her life with security, excitement, and plenty of laughter. I was confident she would make a wonderful wife and mother. After all, I had mentored her most confidently in that role.

When friends who knew that our last child was marrying and moving away would ask, "How do you think you will like being empty nesters?" I couldn't honestly answer. My emotions were caught up in the busyness of wedding plans. But all too soon I knew I would come home to a quiet, empty house, and all the years of nurturing children would be over. When that moment finally came, my heart wanted to feel lost, but I sensed that the nearness of the Lord would not allow it. He still had plans for me.

$\mathcal{N}$EW COMFORT ZONES

I CARRIED THE LAST LOAD OF LAUNDRY DOWN THE HALLWAY that displayed framed portraits of our children at varying ages. Rhonda's high school graduation picture caught my eye. Her dark hair contrasted richly with the bright red cap and gown. She was now a devoted mother of three, with another one on the way. Her family had grown so fast. Lora, our first grandchild, had two younger brothers to contend with, and she was thrilled to know that the new baby was going to be a girl. Although nearing her due date, Rhonda still homeschooled the oldest children. I was glad they lived only five minutes from our house so I could enjoy caring for them when she needed a break.

A few feet down, on the other side of the hall, was my favorite picture of Randy, as a toddler. I could close my eyes and visualize those adorable, short auburn curls and his chubby cheeks, lightly freckled. I smiled as I remembered how his short stocky legs would propel him in a run as his dimpled hands thrust upward, inviting me to hold him.

I paused to study Robin's baby picture, comparing her features to the ones in the picture next to it, taken later with her brother and sister. On my mother's frequent visits she had commented how much Robin reminded her of me. She had my jaw and nose, and there were some similarities in our smiles, but Robin was so much like her father in every other way.

118

Our children weren't perfect, but they grew up knowing right from wrong. We kept the lines of communication open, and they knew they could come to us for help and encouragement. When they failed, they understood that God offered them forgiveness. *Thank you, Lord, for blessing us with such great kids. They know how much you love them.*

I passed Randy's empty room, brightened now with a colorful comforter. Landscape and still-life prints now replaced the autographed pictures of sports stars that had covered his wall since high school. I had redecorated so he and his wife, Debbie, would feel we had prepared a special place for them, as a couple, when they visited from Tulsa. Their three young children were always well behaved when they arrived, but I knew the six-hour drive had to be tiring for them all. James and I tried to make the trip to Tulsa as often as possible to see them and also Robin's family.

Robin's room was next to James' and mine. Her bed was covered with stacks of folded clothing for our next trip. I added the last load to the bed and separated the items that would be put away for a while. I loved our home, even though the sounds of Robison children had been absent for many years. Even in the quietness, sweet memories were here, and I cherished the few days we had between commitments. My decision to stick close to James made our house seem more like a traveler's way station. We were passing through again and again, washing clothes, seeing grandchildren, and repacking. This time, instead of nice dresses for me and suits for James, I was packing our casual shirts, jeans, and tennis shoes for a fishing trip.

James took pleasure in telling our audiences how drastically I changed when I got the chance to be outdoors. "People are shocked to learn that this beautiful, petite wife of mine is my favorite fishing buddy." He would cross the platform to where I sat, take my hand, and gently pull me to his side. "You should see her when we get out on the lake. It's just the two of us in a fishing boat, surrounded by beautiful pine trees. We fish for largemouth bass, and she can't stand it if I catch a bigger fish than she does." The crowd always laughed, and I blushed. He was right, and I had to admit it or he would have kept on with his fun.

Early in our marriage I had developed an interest in James' favorite hobbies. He made it clear his preference was to have me go along, so I was always invited. How many wives have their husbands begging them to participate in their pursuit of leisure sports? I never liked being apart from him, and I felt fortunate to be included.

Fishing was not James' only hobby. He built model

airplanes when the children were small, and though I didn't assist with the construction, I took the kids to watch him fly his models and participate in local competitions. We sat in lawn chairs, strategically placed near the landing strips designed for enthusiasts to land their model planes, and mingled with the other families.

The event was noisy, but we enjoyed watching James fly one plane after another. He maneuvered his colorful models by remote control for takeoffs and landings, then soared them gracefully in patterns that crisscrossed around and often near other models. I wasn't much assistance in the field, other than carrying his repair kit, in case something went wrong. But I was glad to be there for moral support. Whenever one of his planes crashed, James was as brokenhearted as a young boy with a wounded pet as he carried his model to the car.

Nurturing our friendship had been a priority in our marriage. We enjoyed each other's company and purposely found fun things that we liked doing together. We loved the child-rearing years, but we knew Rhonda, Randy, and Robin would someday have their own lives. Even though we did many recreational things as a family, we never neglected our personal relationship as husband and wife. That practice helped us establish a foundation that transitioned us, unscathed, through the empty-nest stage that devastates some couples.

My childhood camping experiences made it easier to adapt to James' outdoor hobbies. However, I never dreamed I would become so intense in the sports we did together. My competitive spirit didn't threaten him; it amused him. He enjoyed telling fishing stories about me, and he certainly did it with more flair than I would have.

We loved fishing for the aggressive bass in the lakes of East Texas. I enjoyed the challenge of putting the artificial lure in the perfect spot, and maneuvering it with a slight popping action as I reeled. When a violent splash occurred near my line, James would yell, "Set the hook! Set the hook!" I knew he wanted to help me when I had a big one on the line, but I liked bringing in my own fish.

Occasionally we planned special trips that included Brother and Mrs. Hale. Fishing was their favorite sport. Even after Pop passed away, we took Mimi until she was physically unable. Her passion to catch the biggest or the most fish gave us great joy.

After I packed the clothes for our trip, I assembled our food supply in boxes and made a list for the contents of the ice chest to be filled the next morning. James always wanted an early start, so I tried to have most of my packing ready the night before. I liked to prepare for a trip in advance. James talked and dreamed for days but usually threw it all together at the last minute. His job was to gather all the equipment and fishing tackle we needed and prepare the vehicle.

When the day came, he loaded and squeezed things into the truck, questioning me the whole time: "Did you happen to see that hat I put on the bed? I wanted to pack it. I hope we've got enough bottled water, 'cause the weather's gonna be hot and humid. Where did I put those new lures I got in the mail?"

We certainly do need each other, I thought, chuckling

as I responded, "They're already packed." I knew he would need them. In traveling with him I saw how focused he became in conversation with people after a service or taping. But he frequently misplaced his Bible or items people had given him and didn't remember them until later. I was usually close enough to keep an eye on him, and early on, took responsibility for the one thing I knew he couldn't be without—his Bible.

122

He would laugh at himself and make jokes about how forgetful he was getting. More and more we sounded like Mimi and Pop. They had lived with us for several years until they retired to a mobile home on their favorite lake. I was always amused when I listened to them remind each other daily of things that seemed so routine. Now we are doing it. Are we getting that old?

James had gray hair at his temples, and everyone said he looked distinguished. When my hair started graying, I immediately began covering it up with my hair stylist's best products. We were grandparents, but we were nowhere close to retiring. I don't think James will ever slow down.

My life had taken on a new pace that didn't fit the grandmother stereotype. There were new challenges as I agreed to cohost our television show. I was terrified when we began the new talk-show format. Before we entered the television studio where a live audience waited, I pleaded, "James, please don't ask me anything I can't answer. Don't put me on the spot. Okay?"

I knew what the producers thought about James' idea of having me beside him. They loved me, but it was their job to look out for the best interest of the show. I imagined their arguments: "Betty doesn't talk. She will never ask questions or enter into conversations with the guests. You will have to carry the show, and she will sit beside you, looking like a potted plant." They were right. I didn't feel I had anything to contribute. James was a great communicator, and his curiosity about people led him to ask questions that stimulated great discussions with our guests and audience. How could I ever do as well as he did?

James coached me. "Relax your eyes and look directly into the camera. Visualize the multitude of people out there who need your help." Each week I prayed intensely, and I put many hours into acquainting myself with each topic and the backgrounds of the guests. I had an agreement with James: if I wanted to make some remarks, I would tap him on the knee where the camera couldn't see and he would smoothly steer the conversation to me. The first time I did this, I saw the red light on my camera flare. I did what James advised and relaxed my eyes as I stepped out with comments and questions from notes I had made before the show. The producers were amazed and encouraged me in the next planning meeting. I gained confidence, and soon James was giving me questions without my tap on his knee.

"The response calls and mail from our viewing audience is begging for more of you, Betty," our director said.

"Me?" I laughed nervously. "Are you serious?"

"It's the truth," James confirmed, "and we want you to host a special show by yourself. You can have all

123

women guests, and I will just sit in the audience and let you handle it all."

"Well, I don't know about that. I just got comfortable being a cohost. I need the security of you sitting there beside me. I know I can depend on you to carry the load or come to my rescue if I go blank. I can't handle hosting a show."

No one let me off the hook—not even God. I put it off as long as I could, and when the time came, the producers made sure I had plenty of outgoing, talkative guests sitting around me at a table on the set. *Hmmm, if I can get through the opening remarks and greeting the audience, then I'll just turn it over to these talented ladies until the floor director cues me to do the close.*

My voice was shaking when I greeted the people. I did as planned and turned the topic to the other ladies, who used energetic humor and dramatic storytelling to keep the excitement going. I laughed at their jokes and spoke brief statements of agreement. I caught the floor director's wrap-up cue and did the show's close with a perfect countdown.

"Oh, I made it through one," I said and sighed. I thanked the ladies for helping me. "Three more to go." Everyone encouraged me, and by the last show I was speaking more easily and entering into the conversation.

For the last show all the ladies agreed that we should invite James back to the set. The camera captured James making his entrance to join us. As he sat at our table, he immediately rallied audience support. "I think Betty did a great job hosting, don't you?" There was enthusiastic applause, and many heads nodded. "In fact I think she needs to do it again sometime, don't you?" As the people clapped, my guests cheered me on. I smiled, thanking everyone for their gracious remarks and encouragement. But inside I was panicked and pleading, *Lord, how far are you going to stretch me?*

CHAPTER FOURTEEN

UNFAMILIAR PLACES

I LOOKED AT MY WATCH AND CALCULATED THE TIME. WE STILL had ten more hours of flying. The direct route from New York to Johannesburg, South Africa, was an exhausting seventeen hours. After the evening meal was served, the lights dimmed and the in-flight movie began. Many around me chose to put on their headphones for a film that had been in the theaters several months. I chose a pillow instead.

Resting on airplanes had never been easy for me, but our taping schedule had been so hectic, I welcomed sleep. I woke up only once and noticed James reading. I knew the five hours of peaceful rest would help my body adjust to the eight-hour change in time zones. James and I, along with our television crew, would face a grueling schedule the moment we arrived at the mission base camp. There was no time to give in to the effects of jet lag.

I thought back to my first mission trip, remembering

the anxiety I had felt on that flight. I recalled the various outreaches we had been involved in over the last fourteen years. Mozambique was first, then Angola, Rwanda, Sudan. . . . James and I had made most of those trips together and had returned to Angola and Mozambique many times. Once again our destination was Angola. We planned to document the feeding programs we had begun in a more remote, impoverished village called Hanha do Norte.

Our last trip to Angola had been the most difficult I had ever made. Reaching the area's most desperate people required several hours of driving on crater-filled roads. We rode in a missionary's vehicle with worn-out shock absorbers and weak springs. To avoid the worst holes, the driver swerved from one side of the road to the other. I braced myself as much as possible, but the long journey took its toll on my lower back. During the trip I had severe pain, whether walking, sitting, or lying down. When I returned home, an X ray revealed herniated disks that required weeks of therapy before I could return to normal activity.

This time I knew the risks and the hardships, but I wasn't afraid anymore—not like in the beginning. I had learned that mission work is not about me and my comfort. It is about bringing hope to people who have nothing and endure great suffering.

Much had changed since our first mission trip to Mozambique, a country devastated by war and drought. Missionaries Peter and Ann Pretorius were wealthy South Africans who owned tobacco farms until they became

Christians and felt the call of God to evangelism. They began a compassionate ministry there after thousands of people starved to death and were buried in mass graves. The couple sold everything they could to establish regular feeding programs and then later, preached crusades to tell the villagers about Jesus.

After listening to Peter's heart-wrenching stories and seeing video footage of the impoverished refugee areas, James had proposed a long-range financial commitment with the leaders of our ministry. They were supportive in the goal of partnering with Peter's ministry but knew God would have to provide supernaturally to begin such an enormous outreach. The next thing I knew we were booked on a flight to visit the South African country we had committed to help.

As we went for our shots on that first missions trip, I had fearful thoughts. The health department required inoculations for several life-threatening diseases. Deadly strains of malaria could be contracted from the mosquitos, and there was no guarantee the medicine would prevent the sickness if you were bitten. *Will we be killed?* I wondered. *Will I ever see my grandchildren again? Will James be so moved by the needs of the people that he will want to go live there?* I had always hoped that God wouldn't send me to the mission field, much less Africa, the one place that frightened me the most.

Many times, as the days counted down for our first departure to Mozambique, I asked James, "Do you still have peace from God that we are supposed to go?" His answer was always a confident, "Yes, beyond a doubt."

In spite of his reassurance, I worried about what might happen. I couldn't hear God over the voices of fear, so I had to trust James' peace of mind and spirit. Off to Africa we went.

The first day, in the village of Pambarra, African children surrounded me the moment I stepped out of the truck. As my heart melted at the sight of them, there was no more room for fear. Their way of life was as primitive as I had imagined, but the needs were more extreme. Little ones, covered in dirt, wearing skimpy, stained clothing worn to shreds, looked up at me shyly. Their smiles drew my eyes away from their rags to the anticipation on their faces. I knelt to be on their level and reached out to touch those nearest me. Immediately others stepped close, with a polite timidity. I could relate to their apprehension but sensed their hunger for attention and affection. After I initiated the personal contact, soon many wanted to hold hands and embrace.

Ann Pretorius pointed out the danger signs of malnutrition. Most of the group around me had patches of orange discoloration in their hair. Several had open sores on their legs, which Ann called skin ulcers, and many had bloated tummies. I realized I was seeing only a few external signs of serious, internal problems.

Thousands of children lined the road as our team set up to feed them a vitamin-rich meal to help fight disease and parasites. I stared at the containers the children brought for their soup—rusted cans, small plastic buckets, and tarnished bowls. When a missionary gave me a small stool to sit on, I asked, "Do we put the hot soup

130

into those dirty containers?" He stepped toward the line and spoke Portuguese to a tall girl. She handed her filthy, dented aluminum pan for closer inspection, and her eyes lowered as she nodded and answered his questions. He patted her head affectionately and placed the container back into her hands. "They bring what they have," he answered simply. "That girl hopes to feed her younger brother and sisters, so we will need to fill it as full as possible."

131

Could our ministry provide clean containers? I wondered. But as we served thousands that day, in only two refugee camps, I realized how enormous that task would be. The feeding program extended to other areas deep into the bush. How could we get bowls to everyone?

Cooking the soup was a strenuous process. Firewood was collected, and women carrying large pots from the nearest creek or river supplied water. To remove impurities, we heated water in a huge barrel. Once the water reached boiling temperature, we added the powdered blend of grains, dehydrated chicken, soybeans, and vitamins. A barefoot woman stood dangerously close to the fire. Her thin arms muscled a long pole in circular movements as she stirred the thickening soup. When it reached the consistency of oatmeal, three other women dipped their buckets into the barrel and poured a supply into the containers at our serving stations. When I was handed a gourdlike dipper by one of the barefoot women, my line erupted with excited chatter.

The first child rushed forward and held out his small, chipped cup with a broken handle. I smiled at him as I took the cup and filled it. A smaller boy crept up and peered shyly around the older boy. His matted eyes and snotty nose told me he hadn't washed in quite a while. In addition, he was probably sick. I knew the children had malaria as often as we get a common cold, and their poor diets weaken their resistance to other diseases.

The two boys walked away, balancing their full cup so none was spilled. *That is not enough for the two of them. Maybe there will be some surplus, and they can return for a refill,* I hoped. Then I looked at my line and saw no end. Once more my thoughts went to the need for bowls. *If each child had the same size bowl, everyone would be fed equally, and we could plan better and feed more. There must be a way, Lord. Help us discover it. The soup is so hot. Our bowl should have a lip on the edge so they don't burn their little fingers.* I was dreaming and hoping to solve the problem the way any caring mother would do.

James served a line about six feet away from me. When a loud disturbance erupted around his feeding station, I turned to see a child crying. James frantically called for help. "Peter, this child held open a plastic bag. I poured the soup, but it burst the bag and splattered her bare feet. I'm sure it's burning her. I was just feeding so fast. I should have known that wouldn't work."

I watched James' pained, sympathetic expression as local workers made a path to rescue the child. As soon as they passed through, the hole closed up again, and the line pressed forward to get their portion. Meanwhile some of the eagerly waiting children around me anxiously stepped out of the line to get their container filled. I stared at their hands reaching out. What would I do if someone gave me a plastic bag? I had nothing to exchange for it if they did.

I began serving soup again, trying not to focus on the container. There were so many waiting. I locked into a rhythm to meet the overwhelming need. There were hungry tummies waiting for their first nourishment of the day—perhaps the only meal they would get that day . . . or the whole week.

As we returned to the base, the sun was low in the sky, framing a colorful, tropical paradise. Peter and Ann wanted to show us their clinic before it became too dark, so we stopped for a quick tour. "There is no electricity," Peter explained. "In about fifteen minutes, the sun will go down, and we'll have to use candles. Our missionaries desperately need light and power for their living quarters and equipment here in the clinic. If we had a generator, we could regulate its use and handle the most important needs."

The larger of the two rooms had a row of occupied beds. A male nurse and his assistant were caring for patients in the other. Outside, down the length of the building and beyond, a long line of women with babies and toddlers waited to see the nurse. As Peter and Ann took turns describing the clinic functions, I studied the group of patient mothers and observed how calm and well behaved the children were. Occasionally a mother released an infant tied in a wrap on her back and cradled it to let it nurse.

Ann shared how difficult it was to get medical help.

"The nearest hospital is located in Vilanculos, a thirty-minute drive if you can find transportation. Most people must walk to that facility, regardless of their condition, and once they arrive, a mission worker provides food and personal care. A bed and first aid are about all they receive. Here at the clinic we might get a doctor to visit occasionally. The nurse you saw treats people about twice a week. When a villager learns there is a medical person coming, word quickly spreads. Women walk barefoot for miles, then wait with no assurance they will be seen. We are asking God to send us a missionary nurse to live here and work the clinic every day."

Ann continued with her delicate South African accent. "Many babies are born here every week. The midwives who assist birthing here in the clinic know how much I love to catch a baby. When we come to check on our programs, I am allowed to assist the women in labor. Of course babies prefer the middle of the night, when we have no personnel on duty. If there are life-threatening complications, we have no trained personnel or emergency equipment, not even an incubator, to care for critical babies. We do everything we can with what God has provided. What little the clinic has is vital to the people in this region."

"How much does an incubator cost?" James asked.

I turned and smiled at him. *He must be reading my thoughts.*

Peter responded, "I will have to research the most cost-efficient way to purchase one, but until we have a generator, an incubator is useless."

James chuckled. "Okay, how much is a generator?"

Upon our return to the United States, we showed the need to our television audience. Gradually we raised the money to give electrical power to the Pambarra missionaries. The incubator soon followed.

While preaching in Canada that year, James felt impressed to talk about the need for a nurse to live and work in Pambarra. Little did we know (but God did!) that a nursing-school graduate sitting in the audience was seeking the will of God for her career. On our next visit to Africa we observed that young nurse functioning more like a country doctor. Physician-type procedures had become her routine. She loved her work and felt God's blessing, though she endured hepatitis and malaria the first few months of her two-year commitment.

On that visit we lived among the missionaries in grass-roofed huts. Our toilet was a hole in the ground with a grass wall around it. We took a shower in a similar structure, where a small amount of cold water dripped from a rubber bag overhead.

There was no stove. Meals were prepared over a wood fire, with bread baked in a primitive oven in the center of the compound. Missionaries homeschooled their children and encouraged them to play with the orphans living at the base. I cringed when I heard about poisonous snakes being killed where the kids played. Thank God, I never saw one!

Getting mail, medicine, and supplies was extremely slow. To make sure it reached the base, most was flown in or caravanned by trucks. Trucking was dangerous;

often the supplies were detained at borders or impounded for no apparent reason. If a missionary became seriously ill, local treatment in Vilanculos was risky. We knew of one instance when Peter flew in to transport a critically ill missionary child back to Johannesburg. "The missionary families endure great hardship. Their safety is a great concern. Even though we provide the strongest medicine to fight malaria, most of our missionaries will get it sooner or later," Peter said. "They learn to live with it." Peter had endured several battles with malaria himself. He had been told that another case could be fatal.

Ann added, "Yes, and it's quite a heartbreak when your small children run a high fever for days, sometimes weeks. That is such a drain on the missionary families. We pray for them and also give them whatever assistance they require."

James and I observed how committed the Pambarra base missionaries were. Although the missionaries had been raised in the comfort of modern Portugal, they didn't grumble about their hardships. They were happy to be in Mozambique because they were fulfilling God's call. They could see the fruit of their labor. They *were* making a difference.

When we returned home, James shared with our family and ministry employees what God had told him during our visit to Mozambique. "I saw the tremendous need among the African people, and immediately I asked God if he wanted me to move there and work with Peter and Ann. God knows I was willing to do it!

But he showed me that he needs me here to plead the cause of the missionaries—to give of my own finances and inspire others to support what they lay down their lives to do every day. He said I would do the most effective mission work by making Christians in America and throughout the free world aware of how much can be done with so little.

"God's Word commands us to give help to widows and orphans. Our ministry has made the choice to be vitally involved in feeding hungry children throughout the world. We care about their souls, but that isn't all. They need food and water to help them survive. We will tell them about a Savior who loves them—the one who gave us life and compassion to reach out in love. I believe we will change the world with this kind of love."

I knew that if God had called us to live in Africa as missionaries, he would equip me to do it. I would submit and trust his power in me to get the job done. But I was relieved by James' decision to stay in Texas and continue the television broadcast. God was blessing the program, and I knew that blessing would extend over to the mission work as well.

James' snoring from the airplane seat next to me brought me out of my dreams of the past. I nudged him, and he stopped. The flight attendants were preparing breakfast, and people had begun moving about the cabin, stretching their legs and forming long lines to the bathrooms.

What lay ahead for us on this trip? Angola was so unpredictable. Everywhere we went, uniformed young men would confront us with AK-47 rifles. Peter was always quick to alert us when he sensed true danger. When our team was stopped at checkpoints, I had seen his ability to discern that something was wrong. When my thoughts intensified about the potential dangers, I chose to pray. I thanked God that we could trust him with our lives, even when we had no idea what we might face.

But the thought of going to unknown places still brought up and intensified those old voices of fear. The last place I had wanted to go was the continent of Africa, and yet that was what God had in mind.

CHAPTER FIFTEEN

UDAN

OVER AN EXTENDED PERIOD OF TIME, FRANKLIN GRAHAM, THE son of evangelist Billy Graham, and founder and president of Samaritan's Purse, had tried to persuade James and me to come see the work he was doing in Sudan. "James, you have got to meet the Sudanese Christians. They are the closest thing to the first-century New Testament believers you will ever meet."

One evening Franklin called again, proposing that James and I stop in Sudan on our way to Rwanda and Angola to visit our Life Centers and feeding programs. He described in detail the work he had established in the Nuba Mountains. "I don't know if you've been keeping up with violence over there, but the area where our mission compound is located has a bridge that is the lifeline to the only medical facility. It has been bombed repeatedly. Thousands in the area are desperate for food, water, and medical supplies, so I have committed to rebuild the bridge with a group of American volunteers. When that work is completed, we will be able to get a large shipment of food and supplies delivered to them." Then he continued, "James, I could sure use your help with this project."

The way James fired back with curious questions, talking over his friend's lengthy answers, told me that he was seriously considering making the trip. I sat listening, barely able to breathe from the anxiety I felt. I didn't want to miss any detail of Franklin's plan. The Grahams' youngest son was known for his wild, adventurous lifestyle before he got saved, but his recklessness had become holy boldness when he found the Lord. The mission work God called him to soon bore the image of his fearless and passionate abandonment. The project he described to James was perhaps Franklin's most dangerous mission in the history of his ministry.

I frequently watched international news and was aware of the massacre of Christians by Muslim extremists in the central part of Sudan. I learned that the Nuba Mountains were home to about 400,000 people who sought refuge from many years of government attacks from the north and specifically those sent from Khartoum, Sudan's capital.

In addition to known terrorist attacks, the living conditions in that region were harsh. The combination of extreme temperatures, steep mountainous travel, and little available water made dehydration a serious problem. Franklin knew the people's survival would depend on mission projects like the one he was attempting.

When I first heard Franklin had gone there to help, I thanked God for his boldness and prayed that he and his team of volunteers would not be martyred like many of the Sudanese Christians who had sought the protection of the mountains. I had heard James comment, "Franklin is a rugged outdoorsman; he's not afraid to go anywhere."

Of course James was a bold and fearless outdoorsman also. He had a reputation for charging in and taking risks. I still had vivid memories of him walking into the middle of the riotous and potentially violent mob in Bucharest, Romania, where the Communist government was in turmoil. So the idea of James Robison and Franklin Graham together in a place like the Sudan, and fearful little me in the middle of them, was beyond comprehension.

I never said a word during their lengthy phone conversation, but I sat near enough to listen in. I noticed James never attempted to make eye contact with me. As soon as he took the receiver from his ear and looked at me, I unloaded my questions with great intensity. "You aren't serious about going into that dangerous area, are you? I would be terrified, and besides, there isn't enough time to get our tickets, visas, and all the paperwork rerouted for such a trip. What area would we fly into, and would you have any guarantee that we would get out once we got in?"

James answered my questions patiently, knowing how frightened I was. I left the room thinking about the challenges we had before us and placed the securing of visas out as a kind of fleece to confirm God's will about our going . . . or, hopefully, not going.

We had so little time that our visa applications, passports, and necessary records had to be sent by Express Mail directly to Washington. James' visa came back quickly, but my passport, records, and application were lost. In fact, when we tracked them, we found out I didn't exist as a person. The government offices had no record of me as a citizen.

"Now, James, you have to admit, this must be a sign from God that I am not supposed to go," I argued. "And with my passport missing, my trip to South Africa is now in jeopardy."

Convinced the mission was God's will, my determined husband alerted our senator Kay Bailey Hutchison and the resources of her staff. My visa, passport, and the necessary papers arrived the night before we were scheduled to leave on an early morning flight. James shouted and praised God for the miracle. "Hey, you're a real citizen of the U.S., and now you have all the necessary papers to go with me. I guess you can finish your packing."

I had started organizing my things in a large suitcase the day we applied for our visas, but it was on the basis of James' belief that we were going, not mine. I still had to finish packing, and there were a lot of last-minute responsibilities for the house to be closed for so many days. I tried to be thankful as I worked through the list, but my fearful thoughts grew larger than my gratitude. My feelings of dread seemed pretty understandable to me. *Lord, if there is a bull's-eye targeted by Sudan's Islamic extremists, we are headed for dead center of it.* I admitted to him that this trip would require baby steps of faith for me all the way.

We connected with Franklin in Kenya, then went into Uganda, where he had obtained permission to fly from their borders into Sudan. "The government of Sudan will not give us clearance to fly in there, and we know planes are frequently shot down, if detected." I listened with horror and thought how a normal person would decide not to fly with that kind of danger. Not Franklin. "We'll just fly below radar so they won't see us," he explained.

143

I flew with a tight grip on James' hand, crushing his fingers the entire way. It was a terrifying but thankfully uneventful flight. As we circled the opening, cleared at great risk for use as a landing strip, I saw hundreds of people gathered below, jumping and waving at us. As soon as we landed and exited the plane, the happiest people I've ever seen quickly surrounded us. They were singing jubilant praises to Jesus for our safe arrival. I moved among them, receiving their welcoming gestures and embraces.

Their physical needs were obvious. Clothing draped like rags on both the adults' and children's incredibly thin bodies. While Franklin communicated with the local missionary, I stood still, surveying all that was around me to grasp the reality of my experience. People who had known nothing but war, death, and torture were wholeheartedly praising God.

I felt the Spirit of God engulf me as their praises

swelled louder and louder. I knew at that moment what James had felt from the beginning. God had brought us to this place. I sensed that I would receive more blessings than I could ever hope to give.

Soon everything was unloaded, and we were led away to the compound. I heard the plane start its engines and turned to see it making its way down the rough dirt strip to take off. Seconds later, as it flew away, I thought of the potential danger the pilots faced and prayed, *Lord, please protect the pilots . . . and, Lord, bring them back in here safely to pick us up.* The very human, frightened part of me wanted them to come back—and soon.

We were led to the camp area, where we met the American volunteers. They were single men and women and several couples, camping in the compound for weeks . . . offering themselves for whatever work was needed. We joined them, staying in some of the most primitive conditions I have ever experienced. All our meals were prepared and eaten outside on the ground, and everyone slept in tents or crude mud huts.

Each day the local pastors assembled with the Sudanese Christians, and the volunteers joined in for a time of praise and worship. Experiencing the Sudanese worship convinced me that serving God was their life's joy. They expressed it with beautiful singing and spirited dance.

Through interpreters James and I heard dramatic testimonies of tragic loss and narrow escapes. But many who shared their sorrowful stories also told of God's great love and faithfulness. We were overwhelmed by their example of simple trust in the Lord.

144

In the first meeting we were told about a missionary who came to their land many years earlier to spread the message of the gospel. He gave of himself sacrificially so that the people of the Nuba Mountains would know Christ and pass the message on from generation to generation. Because of the work he started, many people had become Christians. I didn't learn his name, but it blessed me when I realized that one man's life and ministry had had such an enduring effect on the people. They were committed to carry on what he had begun, believing Christ was the only hope for their nation. The Sudanese believers couldn't speak our language and we couldn't speak theirs. Yet when we gathered, there was a depth of spiritual relationship that felt like church back home.

The presence of God's Spirit was strong everywhere we went as Franklin took us through the compound. The medical facility had cared for ten times the amount of people it was really equipped to handle. We walked as far as we could to peer over the edge of the bridge's ruins. The volunteers were making progress under the leadership of an American who had accepted the role of engineer over a team of dedicated but untrained workers. We found out this volunteer contractor had lost a daughter to cancer recently, and he'd named the bridge after her. Franklin explained, "The bridge must be rebuilt in order to move supplies into the most desperate areas."

After seeing firsthand the brutal reality of their needs for survival, James promised the aid of LIFE Outreach International for several specific needs. He assured Franklin that he would contact him as soon as we returned to the States and could strategize with our mission leadership.

To my great relief the plane returned for us at the scheduled time. Again we prepared to fly undetected. As we were taking off in the plane, I looked out at the believers waving good-bye. Franklin was right. I had seen the purist commitment to Jesus in these people. I had learned a lot from my Sudanese brothers and sisters, who faced danger daily yet totally depended on God for their help. I thought about my prayer the day we had arrived, as I had watched the plane fly away. I had feared it might not return. Now my heart hurt as I experienced what my new friends on the ground must feel when a plane flies away: *Please come back to us. Please don't forget us. Please pray.* I fought back tears as I asked God to help me live as dependent on him as the Christians of Sudan did. I thanked the Lord for allowing me to know them and prayed for their suffering to be relieved.

Several weeks after we left, we learned that the hospital had been bombed and the bridge destroyed again. About a month later, while fulfilling our commitment to Franklin, our LOI team attempted to land in one of the mission areas and drop off medical supplies. The plane was waved off and warned not to land by the people standing in the landing strip. Our team pressured the pilots to land anyway, but they refused, convinced that the warning meant it was too dangerous.

They flew to the next area and dropped off supplies. The following day news came that the entire village where the plane had been waved off had just been destroyed in an enemy raid. The place had burned to the ground, and nearly everyone was killed. We were grateful that our team's lives were spared, but we grieved the loss of those precious believers. My comfort, as I remembered their smiles and their worship, was that Jesus was everything to them. They would never live in danger, torture, and suffering again. They were safe in the loving presence of their Savior.

147

CHAPTER SIXTEEN

*W*ORLD CHANGERS

OUR SIXTH OR SEVENTH TRIP TO ANGOLA WAS NOTHING LIKE what we had expected.

As our friend Peter Pretorius was guided back to his vehicle by the serious-looking soldiers with AK-47s, he stopped by the van where James and I sat. "I can't be sure we will make it out of this one," he whispered to us. My heart began to pound as I imagined the terrible things that could happen to our team and us.

James and I usually went on the mission trips accompanied only by our LIFE Outreach team and the South African missionaries. But now compassionate people from our viewing audience were regularly asking to go along, offering to pay their own way in order to minister to the needy children they saw on our program. Because of the risks involved and the difficulty with housing and transportation in the field, we had not pursued bringing others into Angola with us until this trip. Finally we had stepped out in faith and invited John Bevere, our evangelist friend and frequent guest on our show. John and his wife, Lisa, had invested faithfully in our African missions. For years he had asked to go with us to one of our LIFE Centers in Mozambique or Angola. "I assure you, I am not afraid of the dangers. James, if you can do it," John teased, "then I can do it."

We had also become friends with Bill Epperhart, the pastor from Columbine, Colorado, who allowed us to tape programs in his church after the Columbine High School shootings. He had introduced us to Beth and Larry Nimmo, the mother and stepfather of Rachel Scott, one of the teenage girls who took a stand for her belief in Jesus before she was killed in the shootings. During hours of intense and emotional programming, Pastor Epperhart and the Nimmos told sobering stories that described the impact of the tragedy on the lives of their family and community. James and I were brokenhearted but also greatly inspired by the courage and faith of our guests as they related what God was doing beyond the evil the two young men had committed.

James commented to our television director after the tapings, "I feel that we are to invite these folks to go with us on the next trip to Angola."

After that, everything had fallen into place. And now here we all were, in Angola together, on the last day of our mission. I replayed the reassuring scene I had observed on the two days of remote feeding—John Bevere, Pastor Billy, and Rachel's parents serving soup tirelessly to Angola's malnourished children. Each

evening, on the long journey back to our headquarters in
Lobito, they shared testimonies of life-changing experiences. They told in detail about their personal interaction
with individual children once the feeding was finished. It
blessed me to hear our friends express their joy and
encouragement about the effectiveness of the programs.

No one could have predicted the situation we were
facing. We knew Peter hadn't experienced this kind of
threat since the violence of the war had diminished. As
I glanced back at the other vehicles, the fear of our lives
being threatened swept over me again. I closed my eyes
and prayed. I wanted to shut out the images that surrounded all of us—the many young Angolan soldiers
poking their heads in our windows, taunting us with
their automatic rifles. I wanted to scream at them, "Don't
you know we are here feeding your starving children?"
but I knew they wouldn't understand me.

Only half an hour earlier our team had completed
the largest feeding program in the village of Hanha do
Norte. It thrilled me to see hundreds of excited children
running to our feeding station. Even more, they were
holding the bright orange plastic bowls that LIFE
Outreach International had provided. My dream of
providing bowls for the children had truly become reality, and my heart swelled with joy. Although the feeding
went well, we could hear gunfire in the distance
throughout the morning. Our missionary calmed us,
speculating that the Angolan military were probably
conducting maneuvers in the area.

Before going on to our next feeding spot, we had

stopped under a large grove of trees beside the main
road to eat a sandwich and drink water to replace what
we'd sweated off around the hot pots of soup in the
scorching 103-degree temperatures. Jim Pearce, our television producer, devoured his lunch and a full bottle of
water, then got back to work, changing camera batteries.
By the time the others finished eating, blank tapes were
loaded into the cameras, and the used ones were labeled

and put away. We packed into the three vehicles and
headed down the treacherous road that had caused my
back problems the year before. It was worse than I'd
remembered.

As we slowed down to pass through a gate, a large
number of soldiers rushed from both sides of the road's
thick brush. They swarmed our vehicles, shouting
commands and carelessly aiming their guns at us in close
range. One soldier reached in the window, shouting and
gesturing for Jim to remove the videotape from the
camera on his lap. Jim had just switched the tapes, so he
quickly complied. The soldiers unknowingly received a
blank tape.

Albert Timbani, the local missionary who spoke their
language, bravely exited his truck with his hands raised
in submission. He spoke to the men who quickly closed
in around him, jabbing him with the barrels of their
rifles. After a few moments the soldiers followed closely
as Albert approached Peter, then stopped by our vehicle
to alert us. "Please try to stay calm and cooperate fully
with these men. Peter and I will go and speak to the officer in charge to learn why we were being arrested."

James assured him, "We will do whatever you say, and we will be praying for you."

As Albert and Peter disappeared into the tall bushes, surrounded by a group of soldiers, James took my hand and prayed aloud. Everyone in our van joined with nervous intensity, asking God to protect Albert and Peter and to give Albert favor and discernment as he talked with the military leader. Others voiced short pleas for God's authority to reign over the sinister trap set for us. We all exalted Jesus' name over the rulers of spiritual darkness in the region and in the men who surrounded us. The prayers diminished in audible volume, but I was sure each person, like me, continued praying silently. *Father, we need your warring angels to go into battle for us. Bring us through this ordeal safely and may you get glory from it somehow.*

The men returned shortly, but Peter's report as he passed us hadn't been encouraging. He truly didn't know how we were going to get out of this one. Then, instead of getting into his vehicle, Peter stopped suddenly and faced Albert. Evidently the overt move startled the guards, who shifted their guns to shoulder height. Although their body language clearly was threatening, Peter appeared fearless yet cooperative. He stood submissively, shoulders rounded, acknowledging their authority, then turned his face toward us. As Peter listened to Albert speak and gesture persuasively, I saw an expression on his face that I had never seen before. His thick eyebrows were deeply furrowed. His jaw dropped, and his lips parted as if he wanted to say something to us, then thought better of it. He looked at the ground, crossed his arms, and leaned once again on the door of his truck. He made eye contact with the young missionary, gave a reluctant nod, and then watched Albert turn and head back into the bush, toward the officers' headquarters.

Suddenly everyone's attention was drawn to a brawling crowd of military men beyond Peter's truck. A man, who appeared to be a soldier, was knocked to the ground and surrounded by military men, who used the butts of their rifles to beat him. Others rushed in violently, kicking him on every side. Their anger and abuse shocked me. *If they will do that to their own man, what will they do to us?* I gripped James' arm and looked away. I couldn't watch the mauling that was being encouraged with angry shouts from the guards near our van.

Albert returned with an older man. By the difference in his uniform I guessed he was the officer in charge. He shouted orders to the soldiers, who scrambled to stand at attention. I couldn't see where the beaten man was taken after the orders were given. I wondered if he was dead.

The soldiers crowded into our vehicles and positioned their guns dangerously near our bodies. After the officer got into Albert's truck, Albert motioned for our vehicles to follow him. We didn't know where we were going, but something about Albert's body language gave me hope that our prayers were being answered.

Our van swerved and dodged the huge holes, following the path Albert made for us. I kept an eye on the gun in the hands of the soldier riding in the front seat. I prayed he had put it on safety as our tires dipped into a deep hole in the road. It became obvious that we were going to Lobito. I prayed we were being led back to our mission headquarters, but a crude prison seemed a more likely end if a miracle wasn't in the working.

The crowds of people walking along the road increased in number—a sign that we were near the refugee camp. I pictured the children who would gather, expecting a load of clothing to replace the rags they had worn all winter. Giving them clothing, even if it was used, was something that tugged at a grandmother's heart. I thought of how much I loved dressing my own grandchildren. Suddenly the tears came as I pictured the faces of my precious little ones. Their images came to me, one by one, from the youngest to the oldest. In the graveness of our situation, I took a deep breath and prayed another desperate prayer: *God, please let me go home and see my family again.*

We were shocked when Albert's truck turned into the hilly, narrow streets of the refugee area. Our caravan followed as children came running from every direction, chasing the vehicles. Albert parked, got out, and smiled hugely as he gestured to us to do the same. "The colonel said he will permit us to complete our mission here." In no time Albert was yelling directions to the regular helpers who assisted the feeding program. Large tarps were spread on the ground while we waited on the truck to arrive with the bags of clothing. Guards got out with their guns and encircled the area. The refugees seemed undisturbed by their presence.

155

"The colonel told me that we have been arrested for filming in an area where such activity is forbidden," Albert said. "But as we drove, I told him how I had come to know God through Jesus and how God had sent me as a missionary to the people of Angola. I explained how we feed in that area regularly and that no one told us about the restrictions."

Peter's son, Isak, laughed and joked, "Yeah, like they put up signs saying, 'No videotaping today in this area of the bush.'" It was a needed moment of comic relief.

156

Albert continued. "I asked the officer if we could stop and complete our mission for the day in the refugee camp and he agreed. He says he is a Christian and does not like his job with the army, but he must obey orders. He must take us before his superior officer in Labito when we finish here." He smiled at Jim Pearce and announced, "We can film all we want here, Jim."

I thanked the Lord as we set up to distribute clothing to the children. *Lord, you are obviously going before us. Work in the colonel's heart and give us favor with his superior in Lobito.*

The officer watched as we unloaded the truck when it arrived. The bags of used clothing were emptied onto the tarps as we worked quickly to separate the contents into piles for boys, girls, young children, and infants. There were also many pieces of adult clothing. "Let them take those to their mamas and papas," the missionary instructed. "They love to give gifts to their family."

Once the distribution line began moving past our tarps, I saw the colonel reprimand two older boys for

cutting in line. Shouting in his military voice, he directed
them to the end of the line. You could see the fear in
their eyes as they quickly moved to the back. The colonel had a look of satisfaction as he turned his attention
back to the front of the line.

Within an hour we were back on the road, headed
for Lobito. James was praying again, thanking the Lord
that we had been able to feed and distribute clothing. He
and Peter had found a few minutes to discuss our situation with Albert. All of them knew that there was no way
to predict what would happen, but they hoped that God
would somehow turn it all around for good.

When we arrived at the army officer's headquarters,
Peter and Albert went in with the colonel while we were
guarded once again by young men with rifles. Thirty
minutes later Peter walked out with a big grin on his face
and announced, "We are free to go."

All of our team rejoiced. God had worked a miracle.
We knew we had seen his faithfulness to us and to the
Angolans who depended on our help. Who knows what
all God did in the colonel's heart as he watched us meet
so many needs with the compassion of Jesus. I believe
the whole thing happened for reasons that will become
apparent even more in the future. For that is the way
God works: no moment is wasted when it is given to him
for his glorious outcome. In reality, we went from being
prisoners to having a military escort to finish the job God
called us to do in Angola.

CHAPTER SEVENTEEN

ℒOCKDOWN

THREE DAYS AFTER RETURNING HOME FROM ANGOLA MY SLEEP cycle was still confused with African time. I gave up trying to go back to sleep when thoughts of my day pressed in. It was still dark when I finished bathing and dressed for the events of my day. I glanced at the kitchen clock as my water heated for instant oatmeal. After satisfying my hunger, I moved to my study, which had once been Rhonda's bedroom. I sat in front of the computer screen sipping hot cappuccino between intermittent mouse and keyboard commands. I read the e-mail draft I'd started the previous night, answering Robin's questions about our arrest in Angola. It was a long and tedious story, but I knew she would want every detail of the ordeal, good and bad.

When I was home, I regularly e-mailed family members and a few close friends. I especially enjoyed receiving messages from my grandchildren in Tulsa. At very young ages they had developed amazing skill on the computer and had inspired me to increase my own computer knowledge. With the help of friends and family, I gained enough confidence to do my Christmas shopping on-line. Buying gifts for eleven grandchildren was traditionally a difficult task, so after I succeeded that first year in pleasing everyone with their personal, on-line gift, I was hooked.

I also learned to rely on the computer in other ways. When my mother was diagnosed with Alzheimer's and Parkinson's, I located Web sites and read and printed everything I could find on those diseases. I saved the material I felt would assist me and our family in under-standing what Mom would face as the diseases pro-gressed. I also found resources that dealt with the emotional issues families must battle when a parent or spouse is stricken with the debilitating diseases. The material was helpful, but living it out daily was proving to be one of the greatest challenges I had ever faced.

Just thinking about my mother's situation was trou-bling. *I must get my mind on something else,* I thought. I checked my in-box and saw an e-mail with an attach-ment from a friend. I received many inspiring but lengthy messages from friends—so many that I had a habit of scanning through them hastily to see if I needed to print them to read later or to forward them to the kids. I opened the attachment and read the title: "A Strong Woman Versus a Woman of Strength." As I read quickly, several phrases caught my eye, so I paused and reread them: "A strong woman isn't afraid of anything.

A woman of strength shows courage in the midst of her fear." *Hmm, I understood that one from my most recent close call in Africa.*

I read on, stopping to meditate on the sentences I could relate to: "A strong woman makes mistakes and avoids the same in the future." *Well, I used to live by that one.* "But a woman of strength realizes that life's mistakes can also be God's blessings and capitalizes on them." *I've seen God prove that to me, in spite of my fear and inability to trust him with my mistakes.*

I lingered on the last comparison: "A strong woman has faith that she is strong enough for the journey. A woman of strength has faith that it is in the journey that she will become strong." I closed my eyes and felt the dread of the journey I would make in a few more hours. I confessed, *Lord, I know I am not strong enough for this, but I believe you are making me a bold woman of strength, just like my mother.* I'd learned valuable lessons from my mother's life, watching her lead our family as a strong-willed woman who could face hard times and keep her head up high. But in the last twenty years before her illness, I had witnessed her transformation into a woman of real, godly strength.

In my own life I had first used discipline and determination to make myself strong. But I had lived in constant fear of failing. Over the years, I had learned to rest in God's strength. Each difficulty I faced made me a stronger woman, like Margaret, my mother.

I closed my e-mails and stared at my screen as my desktop appeared with its lineup of icons. I could hear

161

James in the shower. Glancing at the time printed in the corner of my screen, I calculated his getting-ready time for his early morning flight to Washington, D.C. He had an hour and a half before his check-in time. *He always cuts it close on time and I like to be early.*

I collected the things I needed to put in the car: clothes to drop off at the dry cleaners and Robin's Creative Memories family photo book that I was taking to Mom. I had a difficult day ahead of me—one I tried to plan for, but it always threw me. In the two years since Mom's diagnosis, her symptoms had changed drastically and she was now in the advanced stages of her diseases. I never knew what to expect. *Maybe this will be a good day for her*, I hoped.

It helped to have someone go along. Whenever James went with me I could count on his loving comfort. While driving home, we would talk realistically about her condition. He helped me keep things in perspective. But this time he couldn't go.

After dropping James at the airport, I picked up my good friend, Jeanne, who had asked to accompany me after one of our television tapings. Jeanne had known my mother for a long time. *It's been a year since Jeanne saw my mother*, I realized. *I need to prepare her for the shock.*

As Jeanne fastened her seat belt, my cell phone rang. It was James. "Are you going to be okay?" I assured him I was fine. Had he not had to hurry to board the plane, he would have prayed with me again. After ending the call, I commented to Jeanne, "James is worrying about me. He knows how stressful these visits are."

162

During the forty-five-minute drive, I answered Jeanne's questions and described my mother's condition and the care she required. "This is the second place she's been in," I explained. "She deteriorated to the point of needing a lockdown facility, and the one she was in didn't have that kind of security."

"Betty, this morning I was remembering how Margaret would come and visit you for several weeks at a time, sewing and doing all kinds of creative things for the kids. Remember that poodle skirt with the big petticoat that she made Robin? It was so creative. She was an amazing seamstress."

"Mom loved to sew, cook, or help me with a project when she visited us. But then she was that way with all the family. She just made the rounds, staying for a week or two, and then she'd go back to her little apartment for a while. She was visiting her favorite niece in California when she had her accident that seemed to intensify her symptoms. As usual, she was busy helping in the kitchen. But this time she spilled boiling water over most of the left side of her body. She was hospitalized for three weeks. The doctors told us that sometimes a trauma will advance the symptoms, but that she had to have been in the early stages of her illnesses before the accident. So the family all compared notes. Each of us recalled problems with her short-term memory, such as not being able to finish a sentence. And she had been having frequent nightmares that would wake her up. She'd be startled to find out that she was somewhere else in her apartment in Pasadena, Texas—not in her bed. My younger sister, who lived close to her, began getting calls about Mom wandering around the neighborhood. When a neighbor approached her, concerned, she didn't know where she was or how she got there. So we knew we had to do something.

"Sometime after she recovered from the burns, Pete, Marjorie, Helen, and I took turns caring for her in our homes. We hoped the familiar surroundings with people who loved and prayed for her would postpone her symptoms. However, the last time she was with me, her condition failed more rapidly. At least it seemed that way to me. James and I prayed daily for the Lord to heal her. On our television program I shared the pain I felt for my mother's mental and physical condition. We were amazed as our viewers expressed their heartfelt comfort and committed to intercede for her and our family.

"On her good days in our home she might carry on a normal conversation, and hours later, remember nothing of it. The doctors directed us to helpful information on the Internet, and we learned that nighttime was the worst part of any Alzheimer's or Parkinson's patient's day. Mom's sleep patterns disturbed me. Often she would be up all night, searching through the house.

"One cool winter night I sat up in bed, awakened by the security alarm's beep. Someone had come in or gone out. Neither made sense. James and I found Mom in the front yard, wearing her pajamas, clutching her purse. She was demanding that we take her home.

"I couldn't sleep soundly after that night. I would lie in bed listening for her footsteps. Many times I got up and checked on her. I even put a toddler's gate blocking the hallway outside her room.

"After sharing my experience with my brother and sisters, they were all concerned. We talked and decided that for her own safety we would not be able to care for her without professional help."

The traffic had thinned from the morning rush, so we made our way easily to the connecting highways of Dallas. As we headed south, my thoughts returned to the memory of my mother's accident. I pictured her scars from the burns, and my heart ached, remembering how I had not been able to rush to her bedside when it happened. Family and doctors surrounding her assured James and me that she was in good care, but it was still painful to be so far away.

"Betty," Jeanne asked, "didn't you have Margaret in a nursing home near your house at some point?"

"Yes, she was. As soon as the family made the decision to get help, James and I prayed and searched for a facility where I could be near her. We found a place only minutes away, where several compassionate people made the arrangements easier. The caregivers, who knew James and me from our television program, worked diligently to make her living conditions pleasant even though they didn't specialize in Alzheimer's care.

"The transition for Mom—though short-lived—was smoother than any of us anticipated. I think it was God's way of preparing us. Her disease progressed rapidly. One day she passed by the attendants and was through the outside door before they caught her. Shortly after that, several outbursts, one quite violent, forced us to place her in the care of people trained for Alzheimer's symptoms. That's where she is now. It has lockdown wards to keep patients from wandering off."

As I turned into the parking lot, the absence of Jeanne's response forced the replay of my words: *outbursts, violent, wandering off.* I would never be comfortable using those words to describe my mother's behavior.

166

The nearest open space for my car was directly in front of Mom's lockdown unit. I parked and stared at the building that had my dear mother locked in for her own safety. As I turned off the motor, the summer heat seemed unusually stifling. I paused, closed my eyes, and took a deep breath. "I always have to prepare myself before I go in," I explained. "I never know what to expect. She was such a vibrant and caring woman . . . someone who spent her whole life caring for others. Now our roles are reversed. It is like I am caring for a child."

As we made our way from the car to the entrance, I thought about my sister's phone call the day before. "She was doing well," Marjorie said, "and she got so excited when I told her you were coming to see her." I knew Mom could be getting very worked up, looking for my arrival, or she might not remember what Marjorie had told her at all. Alzheimer's patients lose awareness of time—past, present, and future. They slip in and out of childlike phases and forget relationships that surrounded them all their lives.

"She's probably been asking the attendants where I

am since early this morning. She does that a lot when Marjorie tells her someone is coming."

"So you and your family try to give her something to look forward to?"

"Yes we do, but there have been times when she has worked herself into a frenzy, questioning the attendants about her expected visitor. It is difficult for her to comprehend their explanations. Anything related to time confuses her."

The large corridor narrowed to a hallway that ended abruptly before double doors with small square windows at the top. I punched in the security code, and Jeanne followed me. Four patients in wheelchairs confronted us once we were on the other side of the doors. I answered Jeanne's concerned look as we carefully made our way through the area crowded with elderly men and women. "There're always a few around the doors here, hoping to get out."

A woman in a wheelchair near Jeanne pointed in the direction of a frail old man walking four feet away. She was repeating a warning: "No . . . no . . . no." Jeanne moved quickly to the man just before he reached for the large vacuum cleaner leaning against the wall. An extension cord piled inches from his feet would have tripped him had she not grabbed it and moved it from his path. The woman cleaning in the room stepped out and gently intercepted him, speaking in a tone one uses with a small child. We could hear the man shouting at the aide in anger as we walked away.

The lounge for my mother's ward seemed fuller than

usual. I guessed thirty or so crowded into the area, sitting on couches and chairs, but most were in wheelchairs. A small, white-haired man in a wrinkled, cotton robe gripped the wall as a male attendant supported him from behind. I noticed the television was on with the volume barely audible. No one was even looking at it. The residents stared off into the distance or slept in their wheelchairs. Their heads drooped heavily on their chests.

I was glad the odor didn't overwhelm us like it had when James and I visited before. I understood there was little they could do about the problem. I'd witnessed the routine cleaning that was done after a resident's accident. Most patients had no bladder or bowel control. I turned to see that Jeanne was handling things all right; then I scanned the crowded lounge for my mother.

"Mrs. Robison." A nurse approached me. "Your mother is still in her room asleep and probably won't wake up for a while. Last night she got herself all worked up and nervous—then she couldn't sleep. We finally had to give her some medication early this morning to help her calm down and get some rest. I'm real sorry."

"Oh—okay." I stood motionless and then approached the nurse again. "We can still go down to her room, can't we? I'm sorry I didn't call to let you know I was coming this morning."

"You are welcome to stay as long as you want to, and you can try to wake her up if you like."

I led the way to her room at the opposite end of the ward. "They had probably given the shot as a last resort," I said softly. "I pray for these nurses and attendants every day because I know how difficult one Alzheimer's patient can be. They are caring for so many."

We didn't want to frighten Mom, so Jeanne and I entered quietly. My repeated attempts to rouse her failed. She was in a deep sleep, so we began to converse in a normal tone of voice.

I touched Mom gently, adjusting her covers as Jeanne examined a group of old framed photographs decorating the wall above Mom's bed. Jeanne's curiosity about the family snapshots stirred precious memories as I identified the images of people who had been loved and cared for by my mother.

We continued visiting and reminiscing in the small room adjoining the bedroom. I showed Jeanne the creative scrapbook Robin had made as a gift for her "Nanny." I had brought it, hoping to stir the memories that seemed easiest for her to recall.

We continued to wait and talk as Mother rested peacefully.

"Well," I decided finally, after peeking at her again, "she isn't going to wake up. I guess I'll do this all over again tomorrow. I'm so disappointed. I don't sleep the night before I come, and James watches me pull into a quiet world filled with questions of how my visit will go—what state of mind she will be in. Each visit is like losing her all over again."

"James won't be back from his trip for two days," Jeanne remarked. "I wish I could return with you, but I can't. Can someone else come tomorrow?"

I understood that Jeanne had a family commitment,

so I assured her I would bring someone. "Maybe one of Rhonda's children can come with me. You know Lora has come over and played piano for her Nanny down in the visitors' lounge. That thrills Mom because she always wanted one of her kids to play the piano. Of course Mom can't always remember Lora's name, but she loves to see her."

As we walked back to the car, I called my sister Marjorie on my cell phone. Her cheerful voice greeted me, and I began to explain how our visit had gone. I knew Marjorie was celebrating her anniversary, and her husband had planned a nice getaway. When she heard the news about Mom being sedated, she promised to stop by before she left town. Her natural gift for nurturing and her nearness to the nursing home gave her an advantage over Pete, Helen, and me. She'd graciously assumed the responsibility of checking on our mother daily.

"Marjorie," I insisted, "you don't need to go by there. I know you have special plans today. I'll be back tomorrow morning, and I'm sure she will be better." I thought I was pretty convincing, but my older sister insisted that she should at least call Mom.

After dropping Jeanne off, I was lost in the typical thought pattern that followed each of my visits to Mother. I choked back emotions as I wondered how much longer she would be with us. Mom's illness had changed many things in each of our lives. We four kids raised by Margaret Freeman had grown apart as adults. Pete had become a pastor of a Southern Baptist church near Houston, Texas. Marjorie had married a minister;

their family lived in Dallas, faithfully serving the Lord in the Church of Christ denomination. Helen lived south of Houston, happily married to a wonderful Christian man. I married an evangelist and share his passion to reach the world through television and mission work. In raising us, Mom had given each of us a commission with her words and her life. Now her life needs were drawing us back together.

Perhaps that was why we reported in regularly after our individual visits—to feel connected as a family once again. Years before, Mom had made it clear she would not be a burden to our families. She had made us commit to getting her outside care if the need ever arose. That promise had been difficult to carry out, but we did it together. And together we were watching the debilitating phases of her diseases steal her from us.

Giving comfort to each other was a large part of our conversations. Sometimes that comfort was simply a slow sigh on the other end of the telephone. Now, still on the cell phone with Marjorie, I told her, "I really had a tough time on my last visit with Mom too. She wanted me to go find Daddy, because she didn't know where he was."

"Oh, Betty . . . she really asked that? How long has Daddy been gone?"

"Thirty-four years."

The sadness threatened to overwhelm me.

CHAPTER EIGHTEEN

*S*AYING GOOD-BYE

IT HAD NOW BEEN ALMOST THREE YEARS SINCE WE ADMITTED MY mother to the first nursing-care center. Every time I visited her my sadness grew. It was like watching a part of her die right before my eyes. Her memory was going fast. She wouldn't remember me coming to see her the time before. And then, right after I would leave, she would ask my sister Marjorie, "When is Betty coming to see me?"

She was becoming more frustrated and confused. Rarely could she finish a sentence. I tried to reassure her by saying that even at my age I lost my train of thought sometimes too. When she wondered where she was, I would fill in the blanks for her. But it was hard to know how much to say or do. I discovered that it was best not to correct her if she got a date, time, or the name of a person wrong. It just upset her and made the situation worse. And yet sometimes I had to be as firm as I had been with my children when they were young. It was an awkward reversal of roles.

It became harder and harder to carry on a conversation with her. Most of the time we talked about the family. I would tell her over and over again how many children I had and how many grandchildren and great-grandchildren she had.

Although I was glad my mother was receiving continual care, I also felt guilty. No matter how long my visits were, they never seemed long enough. I was hungry to spend time with my mother, since I knew she might not be on this earth much longer. Sometimes I took her out to get a hamburger or a Coke float. Once I brought her back to my home for a visit, but the trip wore us both out. Also, since time is confusing for her, she was continually asking to go back to her room.

I struggled emotionally because I wanted to be able to "fix" my mother, just as I would want to help any family member when something was wrong. I felt really helpless. Doing research on-line and talking with others in similar situations helped. I discovered that there are no pat answers on how to deal with such a horrible disease when it hits a loved one. You can only take it one day at a time, trusting the love of God and your family and friends to share this burden with you.

One friend who helped me was Kathy Troccoli, a favorite guest on our show. During a special taping in our television studio, she ministered through music and teaching. Several weeks later I reviewed the program tapes at home and heard Kathy's heart as she described one of the most devastating experiences of her life—the loss of her father. And soon afterward came the diagnosis of her mother's cancer that proved to be fatal as well. When her mother was in her final, painful days, Kathy would cry, asking God why he wasn't doing something about the situation. God spoke to her by asking her a question: "Kathy, am I not God?" I still remember her stunning words. I found myself weeping before the Lord as she went on to describe how God took pain and turned it into joy. I learned that it was okay to cry and grieve. God understands. As we lean on him, he heals and restores our broken hearts. I realized that I wanted a quick fix for me and my brother and sisters, but God wanted us all to learn to walk with him, even on a painful journey. God spoke to me and said, "I am doing something, and I don't want you to miss it."

175

During this difficult time, God showed me that all I could do for my mother was try to be a blessing to her, try to convey how much I loved her. But it still wasn't easy.

Whether I was away from her or with her, I'd often hear an inside voice that accused me: *But she's your mother. Are you really doing all you can for her?* At times I wondered if Mom would be better off living with us. But then I had to remind myself that my mother was in the best place she could be to get the care she needed. Neither James nor I could watch her twenty-four hours a day. It was physically difficult, and our necessary travel made it impossible.

Yet there were times when my mother would beg me to take her home with me and get her out of "that place."

She would promise just as a little child would, "Please, I'll be good. I won't cause any trouble." And then if I tried to explain to her why she needed to stay there, she would become angry and accuse me of not loving her. She would shout, "I can't believe you are doing this to me!"

My first instinct was to grab her things and say, "Let's go," but I knew I couldn't do that. We'd been down that road before, when she had stayed with each of her children. The only thing that would comfort me, even a little, was knowing that shortly, because of Alzheimer's, she would forget what she had said to me. *But I couldn't forget.* Her words tore at my heart and mind, increasing the regret and guilt when I had to drive home without her.

After each visit I would weep and tell God, "Please teach me whatever you want me to learn through this experience. I want to grow from it." He brought me great comfort through the words of Scripture: *He will not leave you nor forsake you.* I knew Jesus himself was weeping when I wept. And through various ways he continually reassured me of his presence.

I also asked God to make me a blessing to my mother. The hardest part of dealing with Alzheimer's was realizing that the woman I now visited was not my mother . . . not as I knew her. The strong-willed, confident woman was gone. In her place was a confused, frightened, elderly woman.

I truly wished I had the perfect answers of how to deal with my mother, but her emotions and condition seemed to change daily. Each step I took in this new relationship was shaky and scary. But my changing relationship with my mother also increased my confidence in God—and God alone—as my strength and my source. I desperately needed his guidance, his wisdom.

Little by little Mother became less and less responsive. She refused to eat or drink any liquids. Her body, already frail and weak, became more so. She started sleeping a lot, to the point that when I would visit, I couldn't wake her.

James and I prayed continually for my mother, and yet it was hard to know how to pray or what to pray. When you love someone so much, you want to keep her around. Yet at the same time, I couldn't stand to see her suffer and die slowly . . . to the point that she didn't recognize me anymore.

On Tuesday, February 26, 2002, I woke up with the strong feeling that I had to go see my mother. Although James and I always did TV tapings on Tuesdays, I couldn't shake the urgent, compelling desire to go that morning. When I told James, he asked, "Are you sure? You know how emotionally draining it is for you every time you visit her." James was concerned for me, knowing how deeply I was affected by being with my mother now in her changed condition. He also knew how busy Tuesdays were for me, preparing for the tapings that night. But I insisted, feeling a conviction from God.

So I left early that morning, contemplating all the way there just what I would say or do when I got there. As I walked into the nursing home, my heart was in my throat. When I got to my mother's unit, I punched in the security code. I remembered with a wince the time Mom had walked me to the door after one of my visits. It had been so hard to leave her on the other side of the door. After shutting the door, I had turned around for one last look. Another woman, looking lost and confused, was peering out of the small glass window. My heart ached as I thought of all the patients, perhaps once pillars in their communities, who had lost dignity and respect because of Alzheimer's. Once so strong, they had become dependent on others for all their needs, even their most intimate ones.

178

That Tuesday I approached the nurses' station. Then I saw my mother. She was slumped over in a wheelchair, belted in so she wouldn't fall out and hurt herself. Her eyes were closed, and I couldn't prompt any response from her. So I knelt down beside her and said, "Mom, you have fought the good fight. I'm not telling you to give up, but if you want to, it's okay. I love you. You've been a wonderful mother."

Mom whimpered, as if trying to say thank you.

Later I rolled her back to her room, and the nurse helped me get her into bed. As she lay there without any movement, I sat beside her bed. I began to pray and sing. I knew Mom loved the Lord, and she loved music. I also talked softly to her, hoping for some kind of response. But there was none.

Finally I left and cried all the way home. But I knew instinctively that I had done the right thing in going to see her that day.

That week Mother began to lose her strength rapidly. It was as if she had heard my whispered words and decided it was now okay for her to let go of life. It was time for her to go to her eternal home.

On Sunday, March 3, the nurse called and told us Mom wasn't doing well. I asked her to keep me informed, since this had happened many times before, and usually Mom rallied. But the nurse phoned again around 11:30 P.M. with the news that she didn't think my mother would live through the night. James and I got dressed and headed immediately over to the nursing home. It took us the usual forty-five minutes.

As we walked down that long hall toward her room, the nurse shook her head, indicating that Mom had already passed away. Five minutes before I got there my mother had died. I believe that was a blessing of the Lord since I didn't need to remember seeing my mother take her last breath.

As I went into her room and saw her lifeless body, I could feel the separation. I knew her spirit was gone—to heaven to be with the Lord she loved. My tears began to flow. James immediately began to comfort me as best he could. I knew my mother had finished her course; she had run her race on earth well. Finally she was at peace.

I felt sadness, yes, but joy too. Scenes from the past, memories of precious times with my mom, began to run through my mind. I remembered when I was four. Because I had asthma and bad allergies, I'd sometimes have nightmares. I'd wake up in the morning choking and unable to see because my eyes would be matted shut from my allergy problem during the night. But within seconds Mom would be by my side. She would wash my eyes with a warm, wet cloth until I was able to open them. Her tenderness calmed me and put me at ease.

Now at the nursing home, I looked down at my mother and tenderly touched her face. How I loved her. And I knew I would miss her presence every day. But I also knew, without a doubt, that she was now in a far better place.

My mother, Margaret Freeman, died on March 4, 2002, at the age of eighty-one. We had a special service for her. It was a time of celebration for the life she had lived—bringing joy and love to those she came in contact with. It was a bittersweet time for us as we expressed the despair we'd felt watching her become someone we didn't know. We encouraged each other as we reminisced about things familiar to all of us—including the special way she expressed her love for the Lord and to her family. Not everyone knew, however, that she had faithfully given out of her limited retirement income to help the children in our African projects. Others shared how she had given to them in service with her talents. We laughed together, recalling a few of her head-strong tendencies, but came away strengthened and closer than we had ever been.

I have heard it said that the passing of a parent can be a major transition in a person's life, and that has proven to be true. We had lost my father to cancer many years earlier, when Rhonda was only three years old. But I also saw the faithfulness of the Lord through that whole experience, as well as through my mother's death. I remembered how God had told me he was doing something that he didn't want me to miss. *Lord, we've been on this walk for quite a while. Allow what you put in me to flow out to others and show them an example of how you work at sustaining us and how you give grace that is sufficient for every need.*

At the next taping of our program, I let all my emotions flow. I was at ease when the camera closed in tightly on my face. I thanked people for their prayers and assured them that even though my mother had died, God had done a great work in my family and me. I felt the Spirit of God anoint me to share details of my last days with her. As I spoke, I stared into the camera—just as James had taught me—and felt the pain of hurting people. People like Kathy Troccoli and me, who have questioned God's will and searched for some light in the midst of their darkness.

As James sat quietly weeping beside me, I spoke assertively to the studio audience and to the millions who would possibly see the program. "We can put our hope in God because he has a plan, even though the journey looks scary and feels painful." The tears came flooding, and I had to pause to swallow as my throat constricted my words. In the past, that would have embarrassed me, but this time I literally choked out my words with resolution. "More than anything, I want to be remembered as a woman who loved God first. Loved her husband, children, and grandchildren, but God was first."

That experience—and others—has taught me to treasure the time we have in our relationships, especially those in our family, and to keep communication open. During the child-rearing years, James and I made a practice of speaking into our children's lives, through special family meetings in addition to daily praise and encouragement. Periodically James would ask the children and me to bring a pencil and paper to the dining table, and each of us would write down something we were not particularly happy about in our family at the time. Everyone took a turn voicing what he or she had written down, and open discussion followed. Emotions and feelings were vented, bringing healing in our relationships.

However, we never left the emphasis on the negative. James would then request that we all write something positive that we appreciated in each family member. James and I, as well as the children, had to communicate, out loud to the individual, what positive things were honestly felt. The meeting would end with a special time where each family member prayed.

As I reflected on the memory of those special times, I realized how blessed we are to have children who love the Lord and have a strong walk with him. We take great joy watching them parent our eleven grandchildren with such wisdom. They are totally involved in their children's lives and feel a responsibility to set the right examples before them. They have let each child know how very special he or she is to God, and that he is their only source for wisdom and guidance. As James and I spend time with them, we look for every opportunity to reinforce their parents' teaching with positive input.

My family is extremely important to me. But I also

know that God doesn't want us to focus only on our family. It's like Jesus' words in Matthew 5:13-16:

> *Let me tell you why you are here. You're here to be salt-seasoning that brings out the God-flavors of this earth. If you lose your saltiness, how will people taste godliness? You've lost your usefulness and will end up in the garbage.*
>
> *Here's another way to put it: You're here to be light, bringing out the God-colors in the world. God is not a secret to be kept. We're going public with this, as public as a city on a hill. If I make you light-bearers, you don't think I'm going to hide you under a bucket, do you? I'm putting you on a light stand. Now that I've put you there on a hilltop, on a light stand—shine! Keep open house; be generous with your lives. By opening up to others, you'll prompt people to open up with God, this generous Father in heaven. (The Message)*

My new freedom and passion drove me to look beyond my family. I was also able to challenge others to get beyond themselves, to be willing to bring the "God-colors" into someone else's life. Near the end of the television program where I described losing my mother, I encouraged the audience to take the time to see people's pain. "I don't ever want to get so busy that I pass up an individual who needs to hear me say, 'God put some good things in you. He cares about you with all his heart, and he wants to lead and direct you.'"

$\mathscr{F}$REE TO BE ME

AS I READ IN PROVERBS 20:12 HOW HAVING EARS TO HEAR AND eyes to see is a gift from God, I asked him to help me hear, see, and be more mindful of people around me. I knew that so many times I had passed up an opportunity to pray with someone or speak encouragement when I saw a need. I had let time, inconvenience, and the fear of failure or embarrassment keep me from doing what I knew I should do. But now I had come to understand that God sees the whole picture and knows both what I need and what another person needs to help us both grow.

One day as I entered the pharmacy, I noticed a woman standing outside, looking very sad. I recognized her as a store employee who had waited on me before. I went on in and made my purchases, knowing that I needed to take the time to stop and ask her if she was okay. My heart began to race. She was still standing there when I exited. I thought, *If I don't make eye contact with her, I can walk right on to my car.*

That's when I recognized the condemning words of the enemy telling me I had no business trying to minister to her. *After all,* Satan reminded me, *you aren't a very good Christian. You haven't prayed or read your Bible enough today.* Although I had given ear to the enemy's whisperings so many times before, at that moment I stopped. God would not let me pass her by.

As I approached the employee, I looked her straight in the eye and asked what was wrong. She began to cry and share with me some serious needs in her family. Her daughter was ill, and her husband had lost his job. When she asked her boss if she could take off work to get her daughter to the doctor, he had become upset with her. Within minutes I realized that this woman wasn't looking to me for all the answers to her problems. She just needed someone to care about her and listen to her aching heart.

I wept with her and then did something that had never come easily for me in the past, especially in a public place. I joined hands with her and prayed for her. She thanked me and we went our separate ways. The next time I saw her she smiled and thanked me again. She said the fact that I had taken time to pray with her had helped her so much.

Now when I see a person in need, I start the conversation. I let the person know *I* care and *Jesus* cares. I not only say, "I will pray for you," but I really do. As I see God use this new boldness, a gift from him, to touch someone with his love, I am so joyful!

God has truly worked miracles in my life. And one day, not long ago, proved it. Our television staff planned a show where the employees of our ministry filled the audience. They were allowed to ask James and me about any topic they needed insight on—ranging from spiritual, marital, and ethical to personal. I heard the program discussed in our preproduction meeting and realized that I would have no way of preparing what I would say. I quizzed James with my usual doubts about my abilities. "What will I do if they ask me a question I can't answer?" He tried to calm me with the promise of his support, but there were no human words that could settle my anxiety. I recognized that, and in the time I'd normally use to prepare myself for our taping, I prayed for God's insight and wisdom.

The show went great, many people were helped, and I did a good share of the talking. I told James afterward that I felt I had passed an enormous test. In my weakness, God had shown me to be strong. When I trusted him, he was faithful.

When the fear that had controlled me most of my life had left, it was like God had lit a small light inside me, making me feel good about myself for the first time. I actually now believed wholeheartedly the words of Scripture that said, *God has not given us a spirit of fear.* I had learned to recognize where fear was coming from—the devil—and then refused to accept the anxious thoughts that came so quickly to my mind. I would tell the enemy that God said, *When you walk through the fire, you shall not be burned.* At first Satan would simply hang around and try a different approach, but eventually, as I stood my ground, he backed away!

One special Tuesday night we were excited to have the great Bible teacher, author, and conference speaker Beth Moore on our show along with our friend Kathy Troccoli. Both women sat across from me on the set. I listened, spellbound by their gifts of communication. They exuded enthusiasm and inspiration as they shared stories and Scriptures of encouragement. In the early days of taping, I would have sat like a member of the audience, never attempting to break the flow of their inspiration; now I squirmed in my seat, tapping James on the knee and giving little vocal cues that I wanted to talk.

All of them seemed to notice my efforts at once and stopped to make room for me in the discussion. It seemed so out of character for me that James took my hand and couldn't hold back his laughter. I started to make my point, got tickled with the rest of them, and said, "I can't believe I was so excited to jump in and talk." Everyone on the set, in the audience, and the staff behind the cameras began to laugh and then encouraged me with their applause. Beth Moore commented, "See, that is why people love you so much, Betty. And I love to watch this show because you are so real."

Earlier in life I hadn't been able to risk anyone getting to know me well enough to see that I was weak or incapable. I used discipline and self-control to keep my world safe and secure enough for me to handle. It wasn't until God broke through the fear and showed me that pride was what kept me imprisoned in fear, that

I could afford to risk opening myself up to others. Admitting I had needs and receiving encouragement from others helped tear down the high walls that I had built up—walls that had closed me to the truth and had kept me shackled to the enemy's lies.

The change didn't happen overnight. Anytime I was forced into an unfamiliar setting, fear screamed for me to stay where I was comfortable . . . where my small circle of people and situations were in my control. But that's when I had to tell the enemy that I would no longer listen. Instead I had to choose to hold tightly to God's hand and step out in *his* confidence.

189

Gaining confidence came from discovering that I *could* hear God's voice—that God himself wanted to talk to *me,* not just to "special" people like church leaders. Now I wanted to give him plenty of time to talk with me. So in my prayer time I would spend long periods just being quiet, listening to his heart and thoughts toward me. He helped me understand that I would be uncomfortable at times, and that was okay. However, he assured me he would help me keep taking small steps until I could feel comfortable doing what he asked me to do.

One of the things I feared the most was public speaking. Believe it or not, the biggest way God helped me get over that fear was by having me start to pray in public. I never chose to do that, so it was definitely God's prompting. I always shared the things God was saying to me with James privately, letting him know how special my prayer times had become.

One evening, as he was about to close a service,

James said, "Betty, I would like for you to come up and give the closing prayer." I was terrified. But as I approached the pulpit, I asked God to help me share his heart with the people. And he did! From that moment on, in each service I was always a little on edge, wondering if James would call on me to pray at the end. He never did it routinely, knowing getting up in front of people was difficult for me. However, I led in prayer often enough that I became a little less uncomfortable. Yet, even now my stomach still drops because I feel so responsible when ministering to people.

Such situations have shown me that I can trust God to give me what I need when he tells me to take some new steps into unfamiliar territory. But I have to do my part too. I have to stay teachable. And that's something I keep in mind every day. It means handling my fearful thoughts through prayer, changing the messages in my head by reading God's Word to get his perspective and listening to his wisdom. One of my favorite Scripture passages now is Philippians 4:6-9:

> *Don't worry about anything; instead, pray about every-thing. Tell God what you need, and thank him for all he has done. If you do this, you will experience God's peace, which is far more wonderful than the human mind can understand. His peace will guard your hearts and minds as you live in Christ Jesus.*
>
> *And now, dear brothers and sisters, let me say one more thing as I close this letter. Fix your thoughts on what is true and honorable and right. Think about things*

190

that are pure and lovely and admirable. Think about things that are excellent and worthy of praise. Keep putting into practice all you learned from me and heard from me and saw me doing, and the God of peace will be with you. (NLT)

Through the power of Scripture I discovered the truth: Jesus came and gave his life so we could have his mind and know his thoughts in order to live as he did on earth. He wants us to step into a new realm of living, where we allow Jesus to give us the abundant life he has promised in his Word. If we open our minds and hearts, his words will have an amazing effect on our inner selves. They will affect our attitude, confidence, joy, health, and relationships. And, through Jesus' sacrificial death on the cross, the power of these life-changing words is available to anyone who chooses to seek a personal relationship with him. He wants to share his secrets because he loves us so much!

One of those key secrets is the importance of salvation by grace. You see, I did all the right religious things when I was growing up. I was faithful in church attendance, and, by the book of the law, lived a very religious life. I thought that if I didn't, then God wouldn't love me.

Do you believe that? Have you fallen into the trap of thinking it would be easier for God to love you if you are good? If so, you need to know that salvation is a free gift. It can't be earned by our good works—by doing noble or religious acts for God and others. There is no way we can earn God's love and acceptance.

I wasted many years trying to measure up to a standard that Scripture tells us we can never, ever reach on our own. That is because we are all imperfect. Even if you have lived a "good life," like me, you are still a sinner. God says that none of us have met the standard God set except for Jesus. When I saw my own need to receive God's forgiveness and his grace, and accepted Jesus' sacrifice for me, his life began inside me. I finally had the opportunity to experience "life abundantly," as God's Word promises. God planted a new heart inside me, and the Holy Spirit's power helped to set me on a new course.

However, just because I now had a personal relationship with God didn't mean that the old patterns of thinking were magically erased. The thoughts of the enemy sometimes still imprisoned me, locking me away from the real life Jesus wanted for me. How grateful I am now that even as I chose to walk in the counsel of my old mind-set, God graciously used life circumstances to steer me back toward his truth. In my desperation I developed a deeper dependency and an intimacy with him. Through that close relationship, I heard his loving voice tell me how much he loved me. In the warmth and security of his love, I was able to believe him when he told me he would use me to touch people's lives.

When I look back, I realize that for most of my life I had the cart before the horse. I thought I could persuade God to love me if I obeyed him enough and did enough good things. Now I understand that grace doesn't cancel our duty to obey him, but accepting his unconditional sacrifice gives our obedience a new basis of operation. The law of God is no longer just an external set of rules, but a law that sets us free.

The joyful truth is that I have been set free to obey God! Now I can joyfully carry out his plan because I have been accepted as God's child, and he has given me the power of his Holy Spirit to overcome, even in difficult times. I spent so many years working hard to be perfect. But I couldn't do it. What freedom to discover that I could turn the reins of my life over to God, and that it is now his job to perfect me from the inside out!

193

Why is it that we women, in particular, fall so easily into this kind of deception about our relationship with God? That we have to work to present ourselves as acceptable to those around us, including our heavenly Father? Perhaps it's because we have such a desire to be needed. And we spend much of our lives focusing on others and giving so much to them that we lose our own focus in the process. With that mind-set it's easy to count on the person who needs us to be the person who also affirms us. I've learned the hard way, through a long life journey, that God is the only one who can truly affirm us. After all, he's the one who created us and designed a plan for our lives in the first place!

So many women on our *LIFE TODAY* television show tell about their search for someone to love them *just as they are*. And because of that desperate search, they got themselves into difficult situations, including giving themselves in relationships with men . . . hoping to receive affirming love in return. It wasn't until these women admitted that they had a vacuum in their heart, a place that only God could fill, that they could truly be set free.

How about you? Are you counting on others for the affirmation and security only God can give you? In the very beginning of our marriage, I looked to James for my affirmation and security. Then came the dark years in which my normally confident husband struggled through layers of defeat and looked to me for strength and hope. It was terrifying, because I had nothing to offer. After all, I hadn't developed my own spiritual muscles since I had depended on James for my spiritual and emotional strength instead of the Lord. I know now that God used that nightmare period in our lives to make me turn my focus toward him rather than my husband. Because God was our only hope, I ran to him. And I discovered that in his loving arms was the place I should have been all along.

Dear reader, I pray that you too will be able to turn your heart and mind toward God *unconditionally*. If you do, you will discover the reality of the joyous promise in John 8:32:

And you shall know the truth, and the truth shall make you free.

194